Fighting for Life
The Story of Jake LaMotta

Lew Freedman

BLUE RIVER PRESS

Indianapolis, Indiana

Fighting for Life: The Story of Jake LaMotta
Copyright © 2018 by Lew Freedman

Published by Blue River Press
Indianapolis, Indiana
www.brpressbooks.com

Distributed by Cardinal Publishers Group
A Tom Doherty Company, Inc.
www.cardinalpub.com

ISBN: 978-1-68157-022-8

Cover Design: David Miles
Book Design: Dave Reed
Cover Photo: Associated Press
Editor: Dani McCormick
Proofreader: Janette Lynn

Printed in the United States of America

5 4 3 2 1   18 19 20 21 22

Contents

About the Author

Lew Freedman is the author of 100 books about sports and Alaska. A veteran journalist for the *Philadelphia Inquirer, Anchorage Daily News*, and *Chicago Tribune*, Freedman was the boxing beat writer in Philadelphia between 1979 and 1982, covering hundreds of bouts and dozens of championship fights. His previous titles on boxing include *Philadelphia Fighters: The Golden Era of Greatness* and *Joe Louis: The Life of a Heavyweight*.

Freedman's other sports books for Cardinal Publishing/ Blue River Press are *The Indianapolis 500: A Century of High-Speed Racing, The Story of Basketball Great Clyde Lovellette, Cody Rodeo: The Mystique of Buffalo Bill Cody and the Great American Cowboy, Bronx Bombers: New York Yankees Home Run History, The Fifty Greatest Pirates Every Fan Should Know, The Fifty Greatest Tigers Every Fan Should Know, 73-0! Bears Over Redskins*, and *Seventy Summits: Life in the Mountains* with mountaineer Vern Tejas.

Freedman lives in Cody, Wyoming, and Columbus, Indiana, with his wife Debra.

A Personal Note

During the years I covered professional boxing most heavily, between 1979 and 1982 (although there were other fights in other years) in Philadelphia, I wrote about all types. Many of the boxers I covered were great, from Marvelous Marvin Hagler and Sugar Ray Leonard to Larry Holmes and Thomas Hearns. I watched beginners learn quickly just how misleading the word *sweet* is in the description of the sport as "the Sweet Science." There were gloved men who could have been contenders and men who could have been champions but fell just shy of greatness and never fulfilled their dreams of becoming a champion.

There were devastating punchers like Earnie Shavers and slick-moving boxers like Leonard. Yet there was no one around quite like Jake LaMotta. The fury burned strongly in LaMotta. He appeared to battle without fear, and his stamina was extraordinary.

Everything in life came hard for LaMotta, starting in his youth when his family was poor to as a pro when he would not play ball with the mob and was shut out of a title shot for an unduly long wait.

LaMotta's exploits in the ring brought fans to their feet inside small and large arenas. They seemed to understand the visceral emotions he carried in his heart and set free with his fists. In an often-frightening way (especially outside of the ring), LaMotta represented them—an everyman working to make a living. Yet as a boxer, he was one who provided a good show. He was fierce and exposed inside the ring, but that was just peeling off one layer of flesh.

Fight fans loved the way LaMotta gave his all—his refusal to acknowledge that any man could defeat him. Truth be told, outside of the ring he may not have been the celebrity a fan would most want to meet. At times, LaMotta acted criminally on the streets and behaved uncouthly. By his own confessions in written works, he treated his wives abysmally, even horrifically.

Young LaMotta may well have become a casualty of the streets and of his reckless and thoughtless acts, but somehow, some way, he outran his demons, the ghosts that shadowed him, all of his opponents, and nearly all of his contemporaries.

In 2016, LaMotta turned 94. He was married for a seventh time and still making some public appearances, usually in places where he was revered less for leading an exemplary life than for being a legend in his sport.

Even after spending more than nine decades on the planet, it was still not truly clear if LaMotta was a complex man or the simplest of men. Was he defined solely by the punches he threw at other fighters and his many wives, or the battering he inflicted upon himself? Or was there more residing deeper in his soul? Often, *The Ring* magazine took a shot at psychoanalysis when in reality, the job should best have been left to Freud.

When I met and saw Jake LaMotta in Canastota, New York, home of the International Boxing Hall of Fame, he was surrounded by admirers drunk on the one-time middleweight's grand accomplishments in the ring.

LaMotta wore a cowboy hat, a style of headgear he began accessorizing with years earlier, but he engaged in little of the banter he was famous for after his fighting days ended. He took to the stage, where he signed autographs, slowly looping the letters together to spell out his celebrated name.

Several years earlier, LaMotta, then 90, married his girl-friend Denise Baker, then 62. She sat beside him smiling and attentive on this night at The Oncenter War Memorial

Auditorium in Syracuse, New York, as he scribbled his name on the cover of event programs.

At that stage of his life, LaMotta appeared fragile. The last time anyone likely said that about him was immediately after he emerged from his mother's womb. Once a fighter who ballooned up with extra weight between bouts, and later as an actor, LaMotta that night might well have been down to the 135-pound lightweight limit.

Two years earlier, LaMotta was filmed shadow boxing, in as slow a motion as a 92-year-old can muster. It was apparently muscle memory. In Canastota, the fists that had pummeled so many no longer seemed powerful enough to snap his pen in half.

Yet, as the last living boxing title-holder from the 1940s, LaMotta had fooled the world merely by surviving this long. Who would have placed that bet on Jake LaMotta in the late 1950s, in the 1960s, the 1970s?

LaMotta may have been guilty of too many indiscretions to be beloved, but he surely classified as a living legend.

—Lew Freedman

January 2018

Introduction

At birth, the fighter the world would come to know as Jake was given the name Giacobbe LaMotta.

When he died on September 19, 2017, many of the sportswriters who chronicled his lengthy, adventurous, turbulent, and yes, violent and raging life, mostly ignored this name. It seemed like such a little-boy name. The parents who christened LaMotta with fondness as the more benign Giacobbe nearly a century before were long gone, and Jake had long ago set his own course in the world.

LaMotta was born July 10, 1922, in New York City, specifically, the Bronx section of the largest city in the United States. He grew to be 5'8" tall and boxed mainly as a middleweight in the 160-pound class, although he fought several times in the 175-pound light-heavyweight division, as well.

A ferocious fighter whom fans loved to watch because of his aggressive, never-say-die style, LaMotta competed in 106 professional fights. His lifetime record was 83-19-4. Most surprisingly for such an attacking fighter, he registered just 30 knockouts during a career that began in 1941 and lasted until 1954.

LaMotta was known for delivering hard knocks, but he was also from the school of hard knocks—a poor family of Italian descent that struggled to pay the rent, heat the house, and put food on the table. So often, that was the general background of many successful boxers. They were literally hungry as youths and fought with a special hunger to make up for their deprivation.

LaMotta dreamed of winning a world championship and dedicated himself relentlessly to the task throughout

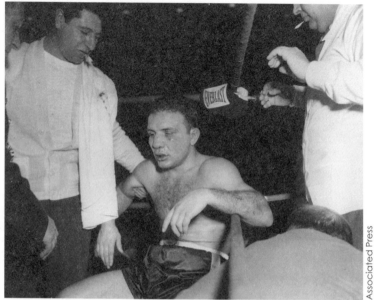

Associated Press

The whirlwind life of Jake LaMotta carried him
from poverty to world boxing champion and ultimately
to the loss of his middleweight title in the ring.

the 1940s. An ear problem convinced doctors to keep him
stateside boxing instead of in the military during World
War II. LaMotta emerged from a pack of contenders for
the middleweight crown, but was prevented from gaining
a shot at the title because he refused to play ball with the
mob, who at the time controlled the sport.

Ultimately, under constant pressure from gangsters and
his own brother, LaMotta caved in and agreed to compete
in a fixed fight, lost it as scripted (if not convincingly), and
received his chance to win the championship. In 1949, he
defeated French champion Marcel Cerdan to become a
world champion, the recognition he was seeking in life.

Over the years, before and after winning the crown,
LaMotta engaged in an epic series of bouts with Sugar Ray
Robinson. The two men met in the ring six times, and it was
widely considered as one of the greatest rivalries in boxing

and sports history. Robinson, called by many the greatest boxer who ever lived, was as stylish and creative in the ring as LaMotta was single-minded.

It is often said that styles make fights, and in LaMotta and Robinson the two protagonists fought in distinctly different manners. They were each other's greatest foils, although Robinson, as befitting his stature in history, dominated on paper. Robinson won five of the six encounters, but they were all close, and even in defeat, LaMotta's stock rose.

LaMotta summoned up a genius of a comment to explain the warfare between the two men, repeating in slightly different forms for years that he saw so much of Sugar Ray and his fists that he was lucky he did not contract diabetes.

LaMotta led a roller-coaster existence. He gained and lost weight inconsistently between his fights, barely making the weight limit at middleweight and then as a light heavyweight. He ate and drank to excess, did not take healthy care of his body except when in training, married early and often, and was prone to rages that seemed to border on insanity.

Both as a teen and later in life, LaMotta spent time incarcerated for different reasons. Over the years, several of LaMotta's wives spoke of him being viciously abusive verbally and physically to the point that they feared for their lives in his presence. LaMotta's marriage to 16-year-old Vikki was immortalized in his autobiography, *Raging Bull*, and the subsequent Academy-Award-winning 1980 movie of the same name. While the film was a searing on-screen portrait of LaMotta's life through the end of his boxing career and slightly beyond, he accrued fresh celebrity from Robert De Niro's brilliant transcendence into Jake from the past. Without the movie and its acclaim, LaMotta would never have been nearly as well known to future generations.

The word *tumultuous* was invented for LaMotta. As a fighter, man, husband, and individual who was frequently his own worst enemy, he was worse to himself than Sugar Ray Robinson ever was to him.

Famed author F. Scott Fitzgerald wrote that there are "no second acts in American lives." For decades, that comment was interpreted to mean we all only go around once. While glibly put, it really is not true for many people. Often people are thrust into situations where they must adapt and change to survive and go on with life. Certainly LaMotta faced this circumstance. At first he floundered, desperately seeking a forum for a second act.

The second act in Jake LaMotta's life eventually came when he left boxing behind. He chose a career in show business, at which he was somewhat successful – to the surprise of many since he did not seem like that type of guy. LaMotta was never a world champ as an actor or comedian, but he did make a living at times on stage and screen. There is no applying the second act theme to his marital life, though. In his 90s, he was on Act Seven.

Truly, LaMotta never left the boxing world behind. He retired from the ring, but not from the sport. He traded on his name based on his reputation in the ring. Always identified as a world champion fighter, LaMotta remained part of the boxing world for the rest of his life. Near the end of his life when his travel was somewhat restricted, he still made it to Canastota, New York, home of the International Boxing Hall of Fame, for its annual June enshrinement event.

It has often been said that home is the place where they always take you in. LaMotta had that kind of late-in-life relationship with the Hall of Fame. He was always welcome there, and his deeds were displayed on walls in the museum. Fans attending the annual Hall of Fame induction ceremony turned back the clock for him. When it comes to sprawling lives lived, sometimes with such intensity you almost want to turn away (and most certainly you grimace at the faults on raw display), Jake LaMotta's seems culled from a work of fiction. In many ways, it was all too real and difficult to digest without Alka-Seltzer. His is one of those stories that, once spelled out, is deserving of the old-time description of truth being stranger than fiction.

1

Bronx Beginnings

No one has said it, but it seems possible that even at birth Jake LaMotta's tiny hands were curled into fists. By the time he was eight years old, LaMotta said, he was fighting for money. His father made him do it, bringing him to cheesy locations where boys battled one another. The harder they punched, the better the boys fared, and the more generously the grizzled men watching threw coins at their feet.

In LaMotta's description of that era of old New York, it sounds as if the bored adults had gathered to watch cock fights. This was simply another version of the battle of the birds. LaMotta's mother was of Italian heritage, but born in the United States. His father was from Messina, Italy, and never seemed quite reconciled to America. Years later, after Jake grew up and gave his father an apartment building as a financial security gesture, his father sold the gift his son gave him, left his family, and fled to his old country. He could make the money last longer in Sicily.

Early on, LaMotta formed the impression his father was a rotten person, and he pretty much retained that viewpoint for a lifetime. One day as a youngster, LaMotta was beat up on the street, and, running for his life, he returned home seeking solace. Instead of consoling him, his father became enraged, handed him an icepick, and told him to wield it as an equalizer. That's exactly what he did, thus gaining a new street rep as someone to duck until the day he forgot the icepick at home and someone bigger and stronger came at him. The only alternative was to employ his fists.

From the first, LaMotta recalled, he waded in and battered the other boy, setting the tone for the hellacious way he fought later in the pros. This power emboldened him. Years later, LaMotta said he got into so many street fights he couldn't calculate the total—maybe the number was around a thousand. If someone challenged him, he fought. It was no big deal to him.

Thoroughly identified with the name "Raging Bull," the fighter had rage coursing through his veins. It was a companion voltage to his blood. LaMotta was angry at the world because his family was poor and lived in a tenement in a Bronx slum. His upbringing represented the opposite of having a silver spoon in his mouth. His father never truly became fluent in English, so he was not in line for any white-collar jobs. At times, he was a peddler, driving a horse and wagon. The family had nothing to give, not even at Christmas. Once, LaMotta said his actual holiday present was a single lump of coal in the Christmas stocking, illustrating the bleakness of his existence as a youth. Later, LaMotta joked that on Christmas his father went outdoors, shot off a gun, and returned saying Santa Claus committed suicide.

There were no hugs or soothing words of encouragement to go around in the LaMotta clan, not for Jake; brother Joey, who was mostly raised at his grandparents' house; sisters Ann and Marie; nor the baby, Albee. LaMotta said his mother was religious, but his father was not. Still, his father made him go to church.

"My father. . . was a really mean son of a bitch," LaMotta said. "If I wasn't home before those church bells rang, he'd drag me up the steps and tie me to the foot of the bed and beat me with that broomstick he'd nailed nine leather strips to 'til my back bled." [1]

LaMotta said his mother screamed and tried to get his father to stop beating him. However, it didn't slow his dad down. Only when she faked a fainting spell did the beating cease.

Jake also witnessed his father hitting his mother, too. His father was impervious to pleas to stop until LaMotta was 12 and big enough to grab his dad and make him stop. Yet, LaMotta held back from hitting his father, an idea he certainly entertained.

On one Thanksgiving holiday, the LaMottas were completely tapped out, and there was no food in the house. Infuriated by this helpless situation, the youth took to the streets and stole a turkey. He told his skeptical mother that he won it in a raffle.

"Being on home relief doesn't do much to keep you warm," LaMotta said. "Everything piles up on you when you're poor. The super in the building doesn't give a damn and God knows the landlord doesn't. So winters I remember wearing as many clothes as I could and staying in bed as much as I could, or in the kitchen, which was about the only room in the house that was even halfway warm." [2]

Yes, LaMotta had parents and siblings, but they were not a nurturing group. The only one he was really close to in the immediate family was brother Joey. The LaMottas thought more about day-to-day survival rather than planning ahead to improve their lot. Sometimes his father worked, but he never got ahead. LaMotta complained that the apartment was cold in the winter, and personal warmth did not fill the atmosphere either.

He did not like cohabitating with rats either. As LaMotta put it, the building wouldn't qualify as a tenement unless rats lived in the walls, rattling around with squeals, and instilling fear in the human residents. [3]

Jake LaMotta was born into rough circumstances in 1922, and except for a few years when he was a child when the LaMottas lived in Philadelphia, he was a creature of the Bronx. Before "Raging Bull" was applied to his name, he was known as "The Bronx Bull."

The history of prize fighting is heavily populated with the stories of men of desperation who fought their way out of indigent circumstances to become world champions, make a name for themselves, and pocket the kind of money they could only dream of as kids when flipping through the pages of magazines.

The Bronx was a hostile environment. It was easy to get mugged walking home from school or at school. If you possessed even a little, someone was always lurking, prepared to take it from you. Sometimes they only stole your dignity if you had nothing else to surrender.

LaMotta's life was every bit the saga of the mythic Icelandic and Viking tales of the past, only set on a more modern stage. His boxing life was led on an epic scale, his fights vicious and extended to the end of the time allotted, his brawling style spilling over to his personal life as if he did not know how to separate the two portions. He seems to have been born that way, not even needing the formal setting of the ring to gravitate to fighting. Long before LaMotta was mentioned in *The Ring* magazine as a boxer fighting under the Marquess of Queensbury Rules, he was known in his neighborhood as a tough guy who didn't follow any rules while fighting. He fought for turf, which was defined as making it home safely.

It is unclear if there are any unpeeled layers of LaMotta's story to investigate. Some stories he has told repeatedly for decades. It was no Disney-like fairy tale growing up Jake LaMotta. His story of his origins as a fighter has never wavered. His father made him fight for pennies and nickels, starting when he was eight years old. Over time, as he became a winner, the boy took pride in his winnings. Sometimes bringing home money to help pay the rent made him feel good, but other times being relieved of his winnings by family made him mad. LaMotta was conflicted about the experience: resentful he was made to fight, pleased when he won.

The fighting venues were neighborhood social clubs where most nights the habitués played cards and drank. Once a week or so, the operators conducted the spectacles of children fighting for change. Jake's father saw a meal ticket in his boy, who occasionally fought as many as three times a week. Raw fighting talent was there, and Jake won a lot of fights.

Occasionally, he won as much as a buck for a fight, which was a big deal to LaMotta.

"Then when we got home, he'd take the money off me that I won," LaMotta said. "Great guy, my old man." [4]

It is difficult to know just what to make of the elder LaMotta forcing his son to fight for coins. These days such events, if they take place, occur under cover of darkness and between tall walls, and would leave organizers and bettors subject to arrest. LaMotta's father also would go to jail for violating child welfare rules. The Depression was just beginning when LaMotta was eight, though, and in some ways his immediate family counted on the money he brought in. However, these fights did not really train LaMotta for a professional ring career.

Very raw in style, LaMotta only knew one way to prevail in the ring, which was constantly using all his force. He fought in this style from his amateur days onward. Those one-minute rest periods between rounds seemed more bothersome than helpful for LaMotta. He would just as soon have kept going for three rounds straight to conquer his foes.

By street standards, LaMotta was a tough boy. It was easy enough to make pals with the other bad boys of the neighborhood. In addition, he also didn't have a lot of scruples. He often wondered why others had more shiny things than his family did, and if he wanted something, he stole it. It wasn't clear if anyone was steering a moral compass for LaMotta.

Certainly, Jake did not find satisfaction in school. He was hardly with the in-crowd, barely showing up for class, thinking of homework as an annoyance—on good days. After a while, LaMotta couldn't be bothered with showing up for school at all. By age 16, he was a public-school drop-out. He was also a criminal, willing to rob on short notice. He wanted to make a score and tilt the balance of the unfairness in life.

LaMotta was not much of a card player, but he played. When involved in a robbery, a heist, or some other illicit method of obtaining money, LaMotta did not always demonstrate the best judgment. He probably wasn't going to out-slick the cops.

He didn't get caught or do time for strong-arm deals or working with others to rip merchandise off a truck. However, the police in the area had their eyes on him. When LaMotta thought about that time period, he said he could easily have been classified as a bum. When he wrote his autobiography, he said his activities would more likely have labeled him a juvenile delinquent. Sure enough, LaMotta got himself into a bigger jam, one where he eluded the police, but which haunted him for decades.

He was hardly a nice kid, but one living on the edge, courting trouble, and trying to find a way to satisfy himself. Before he could sort himself out and dream up a way to make a legal living, LaMotta was nabbed by the police, but not for his most egregious crime. If LaMotta had not tattled on himself or in *Raging Bull,* no one would ever have known that he beat a local bookie nearly to death. In fact, he labored under the illusion in his conscience for decades that he had indeed killed the man.

Of all the jaw-dropping events LaMotta confessed to verbally and in print, none was crazier than his late-night encounter on a dark street when he was 16. Sneaking up on a neighborhood bookie named Harry Gordon who had never done him any harm, LaMotta, shaking with fear due to the irrational act he was about to commit, jumped the man in the darkness. Nervous, LaMotta worked himself into a frenzied state to commit his crime.

The goal was to swipe Gordon's wallet and take the cash to help his family. LaMotta bashed Gordon on the head with a club, and when the man did not go easily into that good night, pummeled him with his fists and left him for dead. He took the wallet and ran like hell, sure he was going to be discovered and arrested. This event in LaMotta's retelling sounds like a personal ordeal for him. Already wild with rage and blood lust for his task, LaMotta could not believe it when Gordon did not tumble to the ground. He kept pounding on the man until he fell.

As his adrenaline subsided LaMotta felt fear, not relief, although no sirens could be heard tailing him. He raced to a local social club and confided in his best friend Pete Savage where they were stunned to learn the wallet had no money in it. Still, LaMotta felt certain someone spotted him, would identify him, and he would be busted. Yet, no cops came around asking questions.[5]

Soon after, a small item about the mugging appeared in the newspaper stating Gordon had died. The article noted the assailant had missed Gordon's stash of $1,700 he was hiding on his person. Everything about this act was futile. LaMotta was angry, somewhat ashamed, and felt stupid for overlooking the money. It did not help matters that his friend Savage taunted him for that mistake.[6]

Miraculously, LaMotta got away with this evil act. He was never taken down for it, but if his own revisiting of the issue can be believed, he was seriously haunted by the assault, convinced in his juvenile immaturity he had killed a man. For years, LaMotta brooded on it. There was no penance he could pay, no way to be forgiven. His misdeed had to remain unknown because there is no statute of limitations on murder.

In his teens, anybody who knew the curly-haired punk who roamed the neighborhood stealing and fighting on a whim, would have bet odds (with bookie Gordon or anyone else) that LaMotta would have eventually gone to prison for murder. He seemed set on that ruinous path. It seemed particularly obvious when LaMotta began brandishing a handgun as a weapon of choice for his thefts.

Buddy Pete enlisted LaMotta in a caper to rip off a card game that featured some dangerous men. He also provided the gun, which was supposed to be for show more than anything else. Possession of a gun seemed to transform LaMotta. As someone who had ultimate faith in his fists' power, he still recognized that firepower trumped hand strength.

"That's what it's about, a gun," LaMotta said. "With a gun, you're the man."[7]

He certainly acted as if he believed it. This was an assignment from higher crime figures that Savage roped him into. They were supposed to find one guy in particular. But revved up, still smarting from his failure to take Gordon's money, LaMotta was determined to grab as much cash from the card game as he could.

At first, when Pete and Jake knocked, they were turned away. They could not breach the door, with the card players saying they didn't want any strangers coming in. On the verge of drifting away, Savage yielded when LaMotta told him to hand over his gun. When he and Savage burst into the card room, LaMotta, sweating so much he said he worried he might not even be able to keep ahold of the gun, took command. He waved around two pistols like some old West gunfighter. He was a bossy thief, arrogant, ordering the players around, even as Savage trembled worrying what his pal might do. Unknown to LaMotta, a couple of mob members were at the table witnessing his wild man act.[8]

After they fled to their social club, the police came for LaMotta and Savage, and, despite the alibi of friends at their club, they were taken to the station. It turned out that the police were after LaMotta because not long before he had attempted to break into a jewelry store. He had run away when the burglar alarm sang, but a couple identified him in a lineup as someone on the scene. Savage was freed, but LaMotta incarcerated. He felt fortunate, though, as no one fingered him for the Gordon attack or for the card game heist.

LaMotta convinced himself getting busted for the jewelry store break-in was a good break. If he went away for a few months, everyone would forget about the bigger-deal stuff. Savage told him he was crazy to cop a plea to the store break-in, but he couldn't talk LaMotta out of doing so.

Given LaMotta's reckless nature, his loss of control in the heat of the moment of robberies, and his street reputation, the police knew LaMotta was no angel. He assumed that this was a first offense, he would be taken off the streets for three to four months tops.

Like much of LaMotta's planning, his logic proved faulty. LaMotta was labeled a juvenile delinquent who showed no remorse for the many errors of his ways, and a judge sentenced him to what he called "reform school."

This so-called reform school, presently called Coxsackie Correctional Facility, opened in 1935 in Greene County, New York. When those in New York City were arrested and convicted, they told their loved ones they were going "upstate." They did not mean to see the sights of Syracuse or Buffalo. They were going behind bars at one prison or another, from the holding pens for juveniles like this one to the maximum-security prisons like Attica.

LaMotta did not outsmart the system. When the judge pronounced a sentence of one-to-three years in Coxsackie, it was too late to make alterations to his thinking and plea. He was going to do time, more time than he expected. As the words flowed from the judge's mouth and his own attorney muzzled him to prevent him from making things worse by snarling something inappropriate, LaMotta fumed.

Getting angry was something LaMotta was very good at. He just hadn't found any way to bend that trait to any kind of advantage.

2

Prison

The reason governments imprison criminals is because man was meant to be free. In the government's view, taking away a person's ability to roam and do what he wants is just about the worst punishment that can be applied. Some men can adapt and cope. Some men literally go stir crazy as soon as the steel gate clangs shut and they peer up at the mountainous walls holding them. They do not respond to orders from uniformed armed men. They resent authority with a mighty passion.

Jake LaMotta was wrong to think he was going to be given a light sentence at Coxsackie. He was wrong to think he even easily might have dealt with a few months behind bars. For a 16-year-old teenager to be sent away after a life of poverty, it seemed to be the final indignity, the last insult, and too much to bear.

LaMotta never was one to dwell on the consequences of his actions. Almost always from the time he was eight years old and battling for the coins, he discovered his fists could extricate him from nearly every scrape or predicament he found himself in. However, this time they could not. Prison was a dead end. There was no imposing of free will. You went along, or you paid the price. If you didn't conform and didn't play the game, your sentence could be lengthened. You had no rights. Oh, did LaMotta despise Coxsackie.

If they watched him closely enough, friends, family, and neighbors probably saw the inevitability of LaMotta being locked up. There was no one in his life who thought of him as a saintly choirboy. Even LaMotta thought prison was the best place for him at that particular moment in his life. It took no time for him to realize his miscalculation.

Jake LaMotta did not respond well to lectures delivered by authority figures. The moment he was admitted to the warden's office at Coxsackie, he showed a chip on his shoulder. He was unable to even try to make a decent first impression because he was arrogant and angry. Immediately, the warden pegged him as a troublemaker. LaMotta received a warning that he had to play by the institution's rules, but a youth who couldn't conform enough to society for his own good on the streets was no closer to being able to toe a line inside.

LaMotta did not play along. He said he never even bothered to smile at the warden—a behavior he loathed to do much outside anyway. The warden took one look at his blank stare, took it for the surly expression LaMotta meant, and taunted him with the phrase, "Another tough guy?" [1]

The warden communicated to the guards that this new prize package might need some taking down due to his attitude. If he only knew. The first hour LaMotta was in the joint, he began plotting his escape. The thought first popped up minutes after he departed the warden's office. This was one indication LaMotta had no idea what he was in for because an escape from such an institution was more fantasy than possibility.

From those first moments, too, as he was being led to a work detail, LaMotta was pushed by the guards. They shoved him around because they could and because the warden hinted he was the type of inmate that might need it. LaMotta never would have stood for it on the street. He would have been in a fight in a New York minute.

When it came to work, LaMotta's idea of making money had been stealing it. If someone nearby had money, he coveted it and sought to take it. At Coxsackie, he was led to an outdoor ditch-digging crew and overheard one guard telling the official on the spot that he needed special attention and should be worked hard. That's what LaMotta saw in front of him—one to three years spent doing hard labor. "No way" was his first thought, as he realized he needed out of this place.

Prison is not really a social environment, and LaMotta so little trusted most people that he didn't even have many friends on the outside besides Pete Savage. He didn't expect to break his normal pattern and buddy up to other inmates, either. He chatted very little and tried to reveal little emotion in his face, something he was practiced at anyway.

"What was there to laugh or smile about?" LaMotta said.[2]

A go-it-alone type, LaMotta wasn't looking to make new friends at Coxsackie, but was surprised when he came across an old one named Rocky Graziano who was serving time in the place, too. Graziano was from the neighborhood, and when they were young, they ran together, up to no good. They had drifted apart during those few years LaMotta lived in Philadelphia before returning.

At least Graziano was a familiar face. Much like LaMotta, Graziano came from tough circumstances. He was another case of a fighter born into poverty who fought his way to respectability in the world.

Graziano's name at birth on January 1, 1919, in Brooklyn, was Thomas Rocco Barbella. He was another Italian stallion in the ring, and he and LaMotta had much in common. They were both Italian, grew up in the same vicinity in New York, became successful boxers, and each won the middleweight title of the world in the 160-pound class.

Graziano finished with a record of 67-10-6, but differentiated himself from LaMotta with his fighting style. Graziano seemed to have concrete hands and blasted out 52 opponents with knockouts. Graziano's father was as overbearing as LaMotta's, making his sons fight one another with gloves on from the time Rocky was three years old. Graziano had more than his share of street fights, too, but initially no interest in becoming a professional boxer. He was not interested in the hard work of training.

When he first tried organized boxing, Graziano fought under an assumed name. To everyone's surprise, at age 18 he won the New York Metropolitan Amateur Athletic Union boxing title. His prize was a gold medal, which he sold for $15. The lure of cash brought him into the sport as a pro.

However, that life lay far in the future when LaMotta and Graziano overlapped at Coxsackie. Graziano warned LaMotta that misbehaving inside would have consequences. His own sentence, he said, got extended because when someone in the big house taunted him, he belted him out.

Graziano sought to offer sensible advice for prison living, but almost from the start LaMotta could talk about nothing besides an escape attempt. Graziano tried to talk him out of it, told him he was crazy, and should not even think that way. He wanted no part of a break-out with him, but LaMotta, who was not the world's best listener especially after his mind was made up, did not pay heed to Graziano's play-it-cool recommendation. Knowing himself and his history of refusing to take guff from anyone, LaMotta didn't think he could do that. He envisioned punching out someone in the yard and being required to serve the full three years of his flexible sentence.

In a savvy bit of wisdom passed on but apparently not recorded in his brain, LaMotta was told by Graziano of the prison authorities, "They not only got all the aces, they got all the cards." [3]

LaMotta persisted. Graziano called him stupid about a dozen times, but offered to help Jake if he tried to run or stow away. The plan hatched called for LaMotta to slide into the back of a furniture truck at the chapel as Graziano chatted up the driver. Through one of his mirrors, the driver saw LaMotta hide and delivered him directly into the hands of the guards. Jake did not even get beyond the prison's walls.

Regular movie watchers understand that when a prison boss wants to add another level of punishment to basic incarceration, the violator gets thrown in "the hole." That's what happened to LaMotta, who also said the guards smacked him around a little as they brought him to his new resting place. Nothing, though, dented LaMotta's anger. Soon after when another inmate hinted at turning him into his "girlfriend", LaMotta broke free of the guards and punched the guy in the face through the bars of his cell. On the street, LaMotta might well have beaten the man to death. In here, he was making a statement. The guards then beat him up. He was outnumbered.

Philosophically, prison is supposed to represent a mix of punishment—society's way of telling bad boys they can't get away with things—and rehabilitation for those who expect to return to society. Recidivism is high, but sometimes criminals learn they will do anything to avoid returning to jail. Sometimes they learn a useful trade that they can apply on the outside. This is especially true if the offender is 16 and has a chance to try and make it in life.

LaMotta viewed prison as an endurance contest, an incarceration he would have to outlast. He was the classic impatient inmate who probably counted the days in his head, if not with Xs on a wall as some movie stereotypes show.

Babe Ruth told people he was sent to reform school in Baltimore because he was deemed incorrigible. He was not in LaMotta's league as a troublemaker. He also received more affection and respect from the Catholic brothers that ran the St. Mary's Industrial School for Boys, Ruth's home after his parents gave up on him. The greatest slugger in baseball history was taken under the wing of a priest, and he was taught baseball, the sport that became his trade when he emerged again to the free world.

At Coxsackie, the prison priest, Father Joseph, reached out to LaMotta who initially was not at all interested in talking religion and trusted the Father about as much as he did other strangers. When Father Joseph approached LaMotta for a talk, Jake practically sneered at him and told him to get lost. Rather than disappearing, the priest invaded Jake's cell uninvited.

Being a prison religious leader is probably less fun than being the spiritual leader at one's own church in the suburbs. The role is definitely suited for a man who welcomes a challenge. Not everyone encountered has the slightest interest in any religion, never mind his own. LaMotta was likely not the first inmate to tell Father Joseph to beat it, either. However, in a facility where the residents are teenagers, such a man might think there is more hope and possibility than hopelessness.

Eventually, LaMotta did open up some, revealing some of his fears, anxieties, and the ordeals he endured at home. At that point in his life, he candidly believed his life offered just two options: fighting or stealing. If those were the only two things he believed himself qualified for, it made sense when LaMotta at last began to see his way out through professional boxing.

After the heart-to-heart talk concluded, Father Joseph told Jake he would help him get started in the prison boxing program. Numerous prisons have sophisticated recreation programs designed to help inmates blow off steam. They are regarded by management as perks, opportunities offered for good behavior. If a prisoner regularly gets into trouble and gets tossed into solitary confinement, he will not be able to compete on the basketball team.

Many famous boxing champions have had prison on their résumé when they conquered the world. From heavyweight Sonny Liston to LaMotta, Graziano, Frank "The Animal" Fletcher; many boxers did time. Lifer James Scott rose so high in boxing that television talked its way into Trenton State Prison to show his bouts. Jake LaMotta, who had been fighting on his own for half of his life, entered the Coxsackie gym to learn how to fight better and cleaner, and ironically, harness what natural ability he possessed to make his style conform to the rules.

Years later after he had worked out in gyms in numerous cities, LaMotta gave the Coxsackie gym a pretty high rating. He didn't know what to expect when he first showed up, but after he'd fought professionally and set up training camps in New York and on the road, he analyzed the gym as being well equipped, especially for being located inside a prison.

Hot-headed, cocky, and reckless as usual, when LaMotta showed up in the gym he believed he could lick any man in the house. At this point, he had no training and his only background was street fighting. There was a fighter in the house with experience, a big guy who was king of the roost. Immediately, LaMotta wanted to take him on. Graziano advised caution, but he already knew how little LaMotta paid attention to his information. Despite LaMotta's pigheadedness, Graziano told Jake to stay away from the big guy who was always knocking down sparring partners in the ring.

Typical of LaMotta, he immediately felt he could take this guy. LaMotta got into a trash-talking match with the fighter, which naturally led to a challenge with the gloves on. Graziano insulted LaMotta repeatedly, telling him he was too hard-headed to learn and too dumb to listen.

LaMotta climbed into the ring against a fighter he considered a palooka. He sadly and swiftly learned he had some serious boxing training to back up his size. At the opening bell, Jake rushed the dude, indulging in tactics that had always worked for him before. He considered himself fast in the ring, but the other man was faster, bigger, and more polished. His foe side-stepped LaMotta and fired away.

For every breath LaMotta took, a fresh punch, a left or a right, or sometimes both in combination crashed into his jaw, nose, and head. The scene did not last long, and the big guy tore LaMotta apart. Worse, LaMotta was in lousy shape for the ring and was soon gassed.

The sparring session ended quickly with LaMotta a mess. He was ticked off at himself, angry at the opponent who told him to go learn how to box before he tried to take on a real fighter again, and through his disappointment he spat fire.

Graziano reminded Jake he had been warned and was a fool to jump into the ring so unprepared. LaMotta finally recognized he had just received an important lesson. He realized his street-fighting background wasn't all that much use in a formal fight setting.

As Graziano removed his gloves, LaMotta vowed that before he was released from Coxsackie he would take on the big man again and whip his ass.

Later, after his pro career was over, Graziano's autobiography, *Somebody Up There Likes Me*, became a big seller. The title referred to the good fortune Graziano experienced in outrunning his difficult upbringing and legal troubles.

In LaMotta's case, he never had anybody really watching out for him. Whenever someone like Graziano tried to help, he generally ignored them. LaMotta learned young he would have to make it on his own no matter what he did.

This time, LaMotta applied himself, helped himself by training vigorously and putting in the gym time, learning the lessons, and sprucing up his game. As word came down that LaMotta was soon to be released to freedom back in New York City, he recalled his commitment for payback. A bout was arranged between the prison champ and Jake. The other man had maybe 15 pounds on LaMotta, much more experience, and the memory of carving up Jake and thinking of him as easy prey only months earlier.

This encounter, however, was totally different. It was LaMotta who dominated on his way out the prison door. His time in the gym was well invested, not only for revenge, either. The experience made LaMotta a boxer and gave him direction in life. Some people come out of prison trained as a welder. LaMotta emerged trained as a fighter.

"I'm serious about fighting," LaMotta told Father Joseph. "I'm going to be a fighter. I always wanted to be one and now I've found out I can be one." [4]

This time Jake LaMotta's judgment was spot on.

3

Fighting for Pay

The fights became real in 1941. Real in the sense that someone was keeping track for the record books; real in that Jake LaMotta was now a professional boxer.

When LaMotta emerged from Coxsackie, returning to a fresh life in New York City, he followed through with his plan to become a fighter. That is to become a fighter officially, legally, in sport rather than fighting on the streets firing punches at people's heads just because they displeased him, as he had done for much of his life up to that point.

Inside the Coxsackie gym, LaMotta applied himself. He worked hard at boxing, learning much about it. He was in much better physical shape leaving prison behind than he had been when he was blowing his top at people for inconsequential reasons or for violence's sake.

There is a difference between fighting and boxing. Famously, writers had called boxing "The Sweet Science." Professional boxing, with trainers, managers, and thousands of fans, is more than just erratic brawling, which is often what transpires on the street.

An English writer named Pierce Egan referred to organized fisticuffs as "the sweet science of bruising" in the early 1800s. *New Yorker* magazine writer A. J. Liebling popularized the phrase "the Sweet Science" more than 100 years later. Some may argue that boxing is more art than science, but the application of the word *science* does give boxing a different dimension than if the sport was simply called punching.

Practitioners of boxing at its best understand the defensive aspects of the game, how bobbing and weaving to stay out of danger is usually equally as important as mounting a high-powered offense. Those in the know recognize a well-placed jab can be as critical to overall success as a round-house right. The jab can simultaneously be a defensive and offensive weapon, employed to keep the foe at bay but also to distract him and set him up, and play head games with him. Some compared a steady jab to the nose and face to the annoying assault of persistent mosquitoes.

By nature, LaMotta was not this type of boxer. He would sooner hit a man on the head with a brick than patiently pick him apart with wear-down punches. He seemed to show no special regard for his own health, wading in with both arms swinging on the attack. If he got hit, so what, he could take it.

For LaMotta to become an accomplished professional, he had to override some of his instincts, learn discipline, and broaden his skills. His innate kill-or-be-killed nature was one thing that could be used. His aggressiveness would always be a plus. But to make it to the top in the boxing world—and that was something LaMotta did point for immediately—he had to expand his repertoire, add weapons to his arsenal, and understand why anyone on the planet would refer to boxing as "the Sweet Science."

LaMotta returned to the same environment he had departed once the prison door opened. His first challenge was not to repeat the mistakes made before that landed him at Coxsackie. Studies show that ex-cons fare best when they have something to look forward to, work at, or focus on. Otherwise, they are likely to make another mistake and be sent away again.

LaMotta had set his mind on becoming a professional fighter. He had caught a glimpse of what it would take during his visits to the Coxsackie gym, and he was determined to stick to the plan. Many other former prisoners taste freedom again with grand plans and optimism, but then things go awry.

"A guy like me," LaMotta told Savage, "the only thing I can do for money is either steal or fight. You know what my record is in the stealing department." [1]

Going to jail made an impression on LaMotta. He hated it, and he did not want to go back. He had not made a good inmate the first time around and recognized some of the worst offenders were probably doomed for life, never amounting to anything beyond troublemakers, lawbreakers, or inmates. LaMotta was not talking about going to college. He was talking about one thing he was good at, developing it, and having it take him somewhere in life. The way he saw things, it was his best option to avoid a life of crime and desperation.

LaMotta selected a gym—there were plenty to choose from in New York in the late 1930s and early 1940s—and began working out, seeking to hone his skills. He said he noticed right away mob figures frequented the gym, too—the muscle men that enforced the wishes of the crime bosses. Even at a time when boxing was in its heyday with wildly admired figures like Joe Louis and only eight weight classes, not everything was kosher at every fight.

There was money to be made by betting, especially when the results were a sure thing. The mob guys required homage in certain instances. In some cases, they guided a fighter's career to the top by providing easy opponents or ones who had been touched by payoffs. They turned a guy into a big name and arranged a smooth path to a world title shot. It could be a rotten business.

One thing LaMotta owned was his pride and he wanted nothing to do with the crooks and fixers. He had been a criminal on the street, but he possessed a sense of honor in the ring. He was one of the men sacrificing his blood and sweat, and he wanted it to mean something. The deserving should benefit in the ring. This was his code. He had no intention of ever wavering from it.

LaMotta's aggravation with the mob began early, when he began demonstrating promise in the gym. Approaches were made to him through his friend, Pete, and his own brother Joey LaMotta. The men in the wide-brim hats with sinister tones in their voices let it be known they would like to manage Jake's career.

Pete joined LaMotta in the ring at Jake's urging, but he did it for something to do. He knew boxing meant everything to Jake, that it was all he had. Savage, the middle man, spurned the mob advances, if delicately. The answer was always no from Jake's side, but that message was not well-received, and the crooks did not give up. They always were after LaMotta to play ball.

It said something for the mob guys' acumen that they targeted LaMotta so early, when he was an amateur. Whether they were laying ground work just in case he became a valuable property or that they truly saw his potential is up for debate. But anyone who knew LaMotta for more than an hour knew that he would not easily be persuaded to compromise.

This aspect of LaMotta's arrival in boxing, and ascent within the ranks, was the most troublesome. For years, the mob figures watched him, worked on him to go along, and set him up for failure if he refused. The crooks didn't care one way or another about LaMotta's pride, nor did they possess any conscience about any ripple effect on his career if he did go along with them. They were kingmakers, but they didn't create royalty for free. It may have been a matter of their own pride for the bosses to show they could control this punk.

Of any 50 kids who visited a gym probably a third of them might have tried to box amateur. They learned swiftly if they had what it took or not. Many might have given up the game after one fight if they learned taking a punch hurt more than they thought it would, or if they were thoroughly outclassed and learned that they were not cut out for brushing off punches. Only 1 out of 50 might become an amateur champ and go on to the pros to do something. The top prize for an amateur was the Olympics, but more realistically for most good fighters, it was winning a Golden Gloves state or national championship. At the time, a major amateur competition called the Diamond Belt was available to Jake, which he won.

For LaMotta, winning that competition was a step. Amateur boxing may help make careers, but it doesn't pay. LaMotta wanted to make his living from boxing, so he turned pro, following the typical early route of moving from three rounds at the amateur level to four-round preliminary bouts on the undercards of headliners.

The short version of LaMotta's style was that he fought the way he lived, going straight ahead. He was not a boxer light on his feet who danced away from punches. He was a slugger who could wear you out. More than most fighters who underestimate the value of such attacking style, he went for the body. Too many fighters fell in love with throwing punches to the head, which could easily be ducked or have less than the desired effect. A fighter who wore a man down by going after the body, pelting his belly time after time, knew that the foe was going to slow down his pace and become vulnerable, recognizing that the war was lost when that happened. LaMotta was good at making that happen.

The four-round fights are for beginners, those getting their feet wet in the pros. Good fighters, guys truly on their way up in the sport, don't stay at that level for long. Four-round fighters do not appear on TV and sometimes are completely overlooked even by the fans in the arena just waiting for the main event to start. Back then, a fighter might only receive $100 for a four-round prelim and out of that money came a share for his manager and trainer.

Making it through four still standing might be a necessary step, but you didn't want to hang around for long at that level. Moving up quickly to six-rounders and then eight-rounders was better business.

Of course, Jake being Jake, and everything about his life always being complicated, he had problems with his first manager and had to sue to get out of a silly one-sided contract he signed. He decided he would rather manage himself, thinking he would make more money.

LaMotta made his pro debut on March 3, 1941. He bested Charley Mackley on points in four rounds at St. Nicholas Arena in New York City. Mackley, who fought mostly at light heavyweight, or 175 pounds, posted a 2-5 record in his career.

Although he gained his greatest fame and recorded his biggest accomplishments at middleweight, or 160 pounds, LaMotta was prepared to take on all comers within a wide range of weights. At various times, in his writing and on TV shows, LaMotta said he probably lost 4,000 pounds during his boxing career sharpening up for fights at different weight classes.

As soon as he made the required weight for a bout, LaMotta went back to the dinner table and snack bar and gained weight back. He did not religiously work out between fights unless his schedule crammed them close to one another. When LaMotta went on vacation, he had no desire to deprive himself of food and drink just because it would make it easier to make weight the next time. His discipline went on hiatus.

This rollercoaster of gain and loss was particularly problematical later in his career when he engaged in championship bouts because there was no flexibility in the weight limits. When he was a young pro at age 19, LaMotta fought guys whose weights also fluctuated. It didn't matter if he weighed 155 or 165 if everyone agreed.

In the beginning of his career, LaMotta fought frequently. His second bout in Bridgeport, Connecticut, took place 11 days after his debut. He topped Tony Gillo in four rounds, also on points.

For the most part, Gillo was what is known as a professional opponent. He had a remarkably busy career, competing in 112 bouts between 1940 and 1951, but it was not a terribly successful one. Gillo's lifetime mark was 36-63-13. One thing managers do when a fighter is starting out is assess his competition. The idea is to face legitimate boxers on paper who in reality may not pose much of a threat to an up-and-comer. Gillo fit that description for LaMotta.

On April 1, LaMotta won by technical knockout over Johnny Morris at the Westchester County Center in White Plains, New York. That arena became a cozy location for Jake. Between April 1 and April 22, he fought there four times, also besting Joe Fredericks, Stanley Goicz, and Lorne McCarthy. Fredericks's record was 4-14-1, Goicz's 16-7-2, and McCarthy's 2-11-1. They are not particularly well-remembered today, and years later even LaMotta had difficulty remembering the names of all the early fighters he faced.

In more recent years, boxers fight less frequently. But in 1941, it was all about staying active, staying busy, piling up victories quickly, and using the numbers to publicize your name. One way to stand out from the crowd was to appear before different crowds in different venues, keep winning, and put on a good show.

In all, LaMotta fought 20 times in 1941, his first year as a pro. After Westchester, he fought in Brooklyn, the Bronx, Queens, Long Island, Cleveland, New York City, and Chicago. LaMotta's attitude was to take on all comers and often he gave away weight in the ring to much bigger men. Fans liked his action-packed style, and so did the mob. However, he would not yield to their requests for management, leading to more far-flung bouts. That is how he happened to journey to Cleveland and Chicago.

At the time, LaMotta's nickname was "The Bronx Bull." The Bronx because that's where he was from and the bull because that was how he fought, charging straight ahead. It was only later, long after retirement, people called him "Raging Bull." The rage fit, too. Intriguingly, neither the Bronx Bull, nor the Raging Bull was a knockout artist. For all the punishment LaMotta inflicted with his fierceness, he did not own one-punch knockout, or KO capability. Whether or not it was because he had small hands, it is impossible to know, but he seemed to possess all the other ingredients of a potential knockout artist.

Usually, LaMotta's bouts went the distance, mostly four- or six-rounders that first year. Other times, he won by technical knockout, when the referee stepped in and stopped the fight because it was feared the opponent might be seriously injured or the foe quit. Only once during 1941 in those 20 bouts did LaMotta win by knockout.

It was on June 23 at the Bronx's Starlight Park in a second fight against his third victim Johnny Morris that LaMotta scored a KO in the third round of a scheduled six-rounder.

Jake won his first 13 fights before an August 5 six-round draw with Joe Shikula on Long Island. Also sprinkled into that eventful year were three losses. LaMotta was 14-0-1 before he fell to Jimmy Reeves by split decision on September 24 in Cleveland. It was LaMotta's first 10-rounder. Reeves, whose lifetime record was 28-17, was bigger than LaMotta, a natural light-heavyweight. The fight was close enough to create demand for a rematch. That rematch took place October 20, again in Cleveland, and again Reeves won, this time by unanimous decision.

Against Reeves, LaMotta experienced a strange sensation in the ring. Even as he wobbled Reeves with a left hook he could not bring himself to up the pace and finish him off.

"I was scared," LaMotta admitted later.[2]

After being pushed around and out-scored for several rounds, however, LaMotta snapped out of his daze, took control of the fight, won the later rounds, knocking down Reeves at the end of the 10th round. This was a case of a fighter being saved by the bell. Reeves had piled up enough points early on to emerge with the decision. LaMotta never again faltered in the ring the way he had this time.

Fans actually booed the decision. Going up against Reeves was a daring move on several counts, so a loss was no disgrace. LaMotta was more middleweight than light heavyweight. Reeves had more experience, and LaMotta had never fought longer than six rounds.

LaMotta's year of living dangerously ended on December 22 with a 10-round, split-decision loss to Nate Bolden in Chicago. Bolden was a major step up in class compared to the other opponents of 1941, even Reeves. During his career, Bolden, who finished 62-35-5 before becoming a trainer, also defeated Tony Zale twice. Zale, like LaMotta, at one time held the middleweight championship.

Bolden won a Golden Gloves championship, but he never got the chance to fight for a pro crown. When Bolden died in 1974, the *Chicago Tribune* cited analysis calling him one of the 10 best boxers in Chicago history.

LaMotta did not make any excuses for the loss to Bolden when he spoke about that match.

"What a pounding," LaMotta conceded. "If he'd been stronger he'd have flattened me. He wanted absolutely nothing but points. Bolden had no intention of mixing it up at all. What he intended to do—and he did do—was let me charge, let me swing, and all he did was jab, dance, counterpunch, duck, hit. He hit me so much I was as much a mess as I've ever been." [3]

Bolden fought the perfect fight for him and taught LaMotta a lesson. Bolden fought the perfect fight for the circumstances. It cost Jake a defeat, but what he learned would be useful later in his career, since he was bound to fight someone else with the same slick style.

As 1941 and LaMotta's first year as a professional concluded, his record read 16-3-1. By any standard, it was a busy boxing year. LaMotta quickly accumulated experience in 10 months.

LaMotta was more convinced than ever that he could hold his own with any prominent fighter in the world within certain weight parameters. He hungered for a world championship and was sure he would one day win the middleweight title.

Two things raised uncertainty about his quest. The first was the continuing shadow cast by organized crime figures within boxing's administration and their keen interest in LaMotta's progress. The second was the bombing of Pearl Harbor in Hawaii on December 7, 1941, which propelled the United States into World War II.

LaMotta went to war every few weeks in the ring, but he might well be called upon to go to war against America's international enemies.

4

Fighting on the Home Front

After the Japanese bombed Pearl Harbor, the nation instantly shifted to war footing, burying isolationist thought as swiftly as the American men and ships had gone down in the sea. There was a patriotic rush to enlist by men of Jake LaMotta's age, men furious at the sneak attack, seeking revenge with a readiness and capability to defend the United States. From December 1941 until September 1945, the country's major preoccupation was the war on two fronts, in the Pacific and in Europe.

Professional sports might well have come to a halt altogether if not for President Franklin D. Roosevelt penning his so-called "green light" letter to Major League Baseball Commissioner Kenesaw Mountain Landis. Landis had written to the Oval Office for guidance, asking whether baseball should suspend operations for the duration of the war. Roosevelt wrote back, saying that although players would not be granted exemptions from service because of their hitting or pitching ability, he thought it would be entertainment and a good distraction for Americans to still root, root, root for their home teams.

At the time, baseball was the preeminent sport in the land, and leaders of the National Football League and the National Hockey League took their cues from baseball and FDR's declaration. (This occurred before the National Basketball Association was created.) The other professional sports leagues continued to suit up their teams during the war, even as numerous players exited the playing fields for foreign fields.

Many athletes promptly volunteered for service. Such Hall of Fame luminaries as Ted Williams, Bob Feller, Hank

Greenberg, and Joe DiMaggio lost prime years from their careers. Williams, who some call the greatest hitter who ever lived, was also called up for the Korean War yet to come.

The fans would have accepted no other scenario. Parents had boys dying all over the world. The image of supremely fit athletes not doing their share was unacceptable. However, much like general members of the populace, there were athletes ruled unfit for service by their draft boards. The reasons varied from punctured ear drums to poor eyesight, from shredded knees to asthma. These men could still make a living playing baseball or football, but would not have meshed easily with a company of other soldiers.

On the surface, Jake LaMotta should have been prime beef for the Army. Yet, he was USDA rejected as 4-F, unfit for service by his local draft board. The reason was a mastoid operation he had performed on one of his ears. The purpose of such surgery was to remove infected cells within the mastoid bone caused by ear infections or ear diseases. The air cells form in a hollow space in the skull.

If the condition is serious enough to ground a potential soldier, then it is probable that being a boxer is not the wisest of professional business choices for someone afflicted with the problem. Fighters are forever being hit on their ears and on the side of their heads as they attempt to duck damage to their faces. Frequently, fighters' ears become misshapen due to all the punches they take on them. The condition is so common amongst boxers that the description *cauliflower ear* essentially grew from these kinds of damages. As far as the United States Army was concerned, LaMotta might as well have been Vincent van Gogh.

Unencumbered from military service, unlike so many millions of other young American men, LaMotta continued to do what he did best—fight with his fists.

After stringing together 20 bouts between March and December in his inaugural 1941 campaign, LaMotta resumed the same intense schedule with the flip of the calendar page to 1942. It was a frenzied pace indeed. During that year, LaMotta fought 14 times. He was in a hurry to become well-known, crack the world rankings, and get a shot at the middleweight title. It's what drove him.

As a person, LaMotta was pretty much one-dimensional, fully engaged in training and official matches, single-minded in his goal to reach the top of his profession. Being a New Yorker, he fought in New York whenever the occasion presented itself. His Holy Grail was to get a fight in Madison Square Garden, which was the place to be. In boxing, the Garden represented the difference between acting in a play in Hoboken and acting in the same play on Broadway. New Jersey was just down the street, but it wasn't the bright lights.

So along came the bouts, opportunities to build his fan base and make his name one that people would remember. Unfortunately, all his early bouts in 1942 took place at the New York Coliseum, not in the Garden. LaMotta had received a taste of life at the Garden once in November 1941. LaMotta had outlasted Jimmy Casa in six rounds, but for most fans, it was a forgettable bout on an undercard.

For the first nine fights of LaMotta's 1942 season, he fought in the Coliseum, which was in the Bronx. He beat Frankie Jamison twice; Lorenzo Strickland, whom he beat three times the year before; Lou Schwartz; Buddy O'Dell; Jose Basora; Vic Dellicurti; Basora again; and then Strickland for a fifth time.

Mostly these bouts served to provide LaMotta with experience and to ensure everyone in the neighborhood knew what he did. On August 28, Jake met Jimmy Edgar in a 10-rounder. Most importantly, this fight was back in the

Garden. In those days, Madison Square Garden was located at 8th Avenue and 49th Street, the heart of Manhattan right on the outskirts of the theatre district.

Edgar, who was born in Starkville, Mississippi, and grew up in Detroit, was a rising middleweight of some substance. By 1946, he was world-ranked. But much like LaMotta in 1942, he was seeking more notice. Overall, Edgar's lifetime record was 36-5-1. He might have accomplished more, but Edgar's career ended abruptly near the end of 1947 when he flunked a physical because he was going blind in his left eye due to cataracts.

When Edgar and LaMotta met at the Garden, they shared the same dream of one day becoming world champion, maybe earning a title right here in this venerable arena. It was a close, tough fight, but LaMotta prevailed on a split decision. This victory represented crossing a demarcation line for LaMotta. He never again signed for a fight shorter than 10 rounds, and he was now viewed as an opponent to be reckoned with. Although he lost a points decision to Basora and drew with him in another fight, LaMotta won all his other fights in 1942.

In the 2000s, when boxers fight more sparingly, a single loss can seriously derail a career, or at the very least slow it. When boxers were much more active as in LaMotta's heyday, the frequency of their matches meant they were more likely to have an off-day and drop an occasional fight. They were not as seriously punished for a defeat then in fans' consideration or in the rankings.

LaMotta was of a mind that he would fight anyone, any time, even if the opponent was larger than middleweight. He wanted to stay active, make money, and pile up victories. At a time when African-American fighters were discriminated against, LaMotta was an equal-opportunity puncher. He did not care about the color of the man's skin in the opposite corner. He took on all comers.

Edgar was black. Basora (whose career record was 78-20-7) was Puerto Rican. LaMotta didn't care who his opponents were. To him, the dark-skinned fighters were just guys.

Joe Louis was the heavyweight champion from 1937 to 1949. He was the first African American to win that title since Jack Johnson. Johnson faced incredible discrimination after he captured the crown in 1908. "The Galveston Giant" was forced to fight overseas. He faced trumped-up legal charges. His outgoing personality, propensity for dating white women and then marrying one, made him a pariah to the white establishment, which hounded him. Johnson never did anything wrong besides living what was considered a brash lifestyle.

Louis's handlers learned from the world's cruelties heaped on Johnson. They guided Louis to the top carefully. He was instructed never to smile while standing over a downed white opponent. He was told to be polite, be careful where he was seen in public, and be cautious of what he did in public. Louis was less flamboyant than Johnson, anyway. By his dignity and demeanor, he single-handedly improved race relations across the country, though one man alone was not going to cure society's ills.

Also, when the Army called on Louis, he entered the service as a private, deflecting the chance to become an officer. He visibly and actively raised money for the cause, sold war bonds, and entertained troops. In a dramatic moment, Louis, who was not renowned as an eloquent speaker, made a speech at a Navy relief fund-raising dinner and uttered a phrase that resonated across the land. He said the U.S. would win the war. "We can't lose because God's on our side," Louis said.

Initially, some people thought Louis got it backwards, that he really should have said Americans were on God's side. Then his statement took hold and columnists declared that Louis had named the war. Giving up lucrative paydays during war-time, raising money for the war effort, and basically just being Joe Louis, the good man he had always been, increased Louis's stature.

Widely acclaimed as a hero to African Americans before that, Louis gained millions more followers across ethnic and color lines. What he could not do, however, was provide opportunities for other African American fighters when local promoters held them down. Unlike a presidential election when the candidate at the top of the ballot sometimes has coattails that drag others in state elections to victory, Louis did not have that sway.

LaMotta, who was constantly under scrutiny by the mob and regularly put under pressure to sign his managerial rights over to gangsters, understood the prejudice against African American fighters. If the squeeze on LaMotta was behind the scenes, it was clear to many that African Americans were squeezed out of the picture at lightweight, welterweight, and middleweight levels just because of their skin color. They had trouble getting good-paying fights and were denied chances to fight for titles.

Jake knew the plight of African American fighters. He was on no mission to right wrongs, but if he thought the guy was an appropriate opponent and would help produce a good gate, he didn't care about skin color.

LaMotta's fight after Edgar was against Dellicurti, a tough pro from New York who built a 40-33-9 record by ducking no one during his career. The bout went the full 10 rounds at the Coliseum in the Bronx, and served as a bridge to the next phase of LaMotta's career.

It set the stage for one of the most famous and brutal rivalries in sport. On October 2, 1942, LaMotta encountered Sugar Ray Robinson in a boxing ring for the first time at Madison Square Garden. It was the first of six epic matches between the two men who were after the same thing, a world title.

Most boxing experts credit Robinson as being the best pound-for-pound fighter who ever lived. He and Muhammad Ali are considered the greatest professional fighters of all-time, with Louis right there on most lists. Like those two other men, Robinson was African American. The success and guidance of Louis helped Robinson in the early stages of his career.

Robinson, born in 1921, was a child of the South. His birth place was Ailey, Georgia, and his name at the time was Walker Smith Jr. He was a member of a family that was part of the Great Migration that saw millions of black people escape southern prejudice by moving to the large northern cities for jobs and more freedoms.

The Robinson family chose Detroit as a landing spot, although when Walker Smith Sr. surrendered family duties, his son was dragged back to Georgia for a year by his mother Leila. Unable to make enough money to support the family in Georgia, which included two daughters, Leila Smith moved to New York to be near other relatives. Once there, she made sure the kids kept active, and young Walter was sent to a recreation center to stay busy and out of trouble. There he could swim, play checkers, basketball, and box.

Then, the Smiths moved to Harlem. It was the Great Depression, but this was the period described as the Harlem Renaissance, when African American culture was in full bloom in that corner of New York.

Boxing is what made Robinson. It resulted in a name change and ultimately worldwide fame. The culture also dramatically shaped him.

These aspects of his life were all part of the Sugar Ray narrative, as integral to the man's accomplishments, style, and manner as LaMotta's time as a petty thief and time spent incarcerated at Coxsackie was to him. But when LaMotta and Robinson battled for the first time at the Garden, not so much was known about either of them other than they represented promise in the sport of boxing.

No one imagined the men would stretch one of the greatest rivalries in American sport across nine years.

5

Jake's New Best Enemy

Jake LaMotta was seeking an opportunity to fight for the middleweight title. He had built a following in New York, the epicenter of boxing, with his frequent appearances and take-no-prisoners style, and he was collecting victories. What he needed was a triumph over a big name, another contender, someone whose status was equal or superior to his own so that he could no longer be ignored. That's how LaMotta's thinking went in the early 1940s and in a perfect world he would have been correct. He did not completely realize the stranglehold the mob had over his future. LaMotta could go to Cleveland and beat anyone he wanted, and he could beat as many people as he wanted, but that would not necessarily guarantee him a shot at the crown.

LaMotta needed a showcase win. Opportunity arose in October of 1942 when LaMotta met Sugar Ray Robinson for the first time at Madison Square Garden. At that time, there was no way LaMotta could imagine his in-the-ring relationship with Robinson, which went on for nearly a decade, would be longer than some of his marriages. Nor would Jake, or anybody else at the time, ever have envisioned their two names being linked together forever in boxing annals. That year they were both in their early twenties, optimistic about life, and still reaching for their goals. They happened to have the same major goal, winning a championship. Interestingly, LaMotta could readily move up to light heavyweight (175 lbs), and Robinson often fought at welterweight (147 lbs). They met in the middle at middleweight.

Robinson's professional record was 35-0 at the time. He had beaten Fritzie Zivic and Sammy Angott twice each.

Zivic, primarily a middleweight, compiled a record of 158-65-9, and Angott's career record was 94-29-8. These were not guys you looked past. At any time, either of them could clock you and put you out of business. Before either LaMotta or Robinson owned a world title, Zivic was the welterweight champ.

When LaMotta and Robinson signed for their first bout, the weight limits were loose. It was almost as if they had been plucked off a playground by a teacher and told to mix it up because they appeared roughly the same size. LaMotta weighed 157 pounds for the bout and Robinson 145. The only weight disparity where such a spread usually comes into play is heavyweight.

Neither man would have given a single thought to the likelihood they were beginning a series of dramatic engagements that has only ever been eclipsed as a notable rivalry in the sport by Muhammad Ali–Joe Frazier showdowns. At the time, they were more of a mind to just have their seconds put some new face in front of them before moving on.

They were very different men, although both came from poverty. The contrasts were more distinct than the similarities, starting with LaMotta being white and Robinson black. They were both from New York City, but grew up worlds apart in the Bronx and Harlem. LaMotta, at that stage of his life, was no snappy dresser. Robinson preened in the mirror before stepping into the street to make sure he always looked his absolute best. In the ring, LaMotta was a brawler, while Robinson a dancer. LaMotta charged straight ahead, while Robinson would stick and move.

LaMotta probably did not know that much about Robinson before their first bout. He would, though, come to learn about the main foe of his career in and out of the ring. For that matter, as Robinson's longevity and prominence grew, America came to learn much more about him as well.

As Robinson's career and life unfolded, he became a hero to the African American community, the linear (if not weight class) descendent of Joe Louis as a boxing figure. Later, he morphed into a star, appreciated as probably the most singularly talented boxer in history at any weight class. Robinson's fame spread from local star to national superstar to legendary icon.

Except for the long list of LaMotta's wives (and his children), it can easily be argued that Robinson was the most important person in his life. At the very least, Robinson was the most important individual of LaMotta's career. While they did not dislike one another, it was not because they were best friends. They were best opponents.

"There's a curious relationship there," LaMotta once said. "In one sense he was the only guy I was never able to nail the way I wanted to nail. He was a nemesis to me. But on the other hand, his reputation was built on the fact that he had beaten me." [1]

Later in life, once he realized that the comment would always bring a laugh, LaMotta said, "I fought Sugar Ray so many times it's a wonder I didn't get diabetes." He uttered a close variation of that line many times over in many forums, on the stage, television, or in press conferences.

Sugar Ray Robinson possessed a style LaMotta could never master in the ring. He was an artist, with hands so quick they could deliver a punch as a blur, feet so swift he might as well have been dancing at Small's Paradise or Minton's Playhouse. Yet, he also had deadly power in his fists. If any boxer was ever the complete package, it was Robinson.

After the family's early poverty in Georgia, Detroit, and Harlem, Robinson very desperately sought success, to always have folding money in his pocket, and be the Man when he walked in the door of a hopping place. Robinson loved being the center of attention. From the time he was young and stood out at his boxing club, he hungered to not only be the best, but use his skills to obtain fine things. He sought to absorb culture and was passionate about jazz and other music. If Robinson had the talent (he had some, but not enough to make it big), he would have forsaken the ring altogether to become a traveling entertainer (he tried it, but failed). Robinson is not remembered today as someone who could carry a tune, but as someone who could pack a wallop. It was his affinity for boxing that made him famous and keeps him famous today.

The first step in the evolution of a poor African American youngster into a world champion occurred when he visited New York's Salem Crescent Athletic Club for the first time when he was 13. It was an offshoot of the Salem Methodist Episcopal Church where the elders believed that sports could save young lives. The church developed a magnificent boxing program and Robinson became the star pupil.

When he first became old enough to run around his neighborhood, Robinson was as much at risk of getting into trouble as any of his friends. Before entering the gym, the closest the boy had come to Salem Methodist was playing dice games in the alley next to the building. Robinson had bragged to his friends that he had met Joe Louis once in Detroit (which was true), but they didn't believe him. Who knew one day he would be compared to him, and favorably at that?

The trainer of the Salem boxing team was George Gainford. He was an adult father figure and knew his stuff in the gym. He dreamed of finding and developing a young fighter who could blossom into a potential champion. Robinson flashed early notable skills, but it took some time for him to polish them.

The boys in the gym aspired to show off their abilities in the local amateur tournaments. There were so many of them, though, there wasn't enough room for all of them every time in a limited number of weight classes. Robinson wasn't even first string when Salem entered Amateur Athletic Union (AAU) tournaments. Although Robinson regularly lobbied for a chance, essentially, he was on the bench.

That changed one night when the Salem team was in Kingston, New York, for an event and the local promoter informed Gainford he was looking for a flyweight opponent. The amateur flyweight class is for those who weigh between 108 and 115 pounds. Gainford told the other man he did not have anyone on his team at that weight. Robinson begged for a chance and Gainford agreed, but there was one obstacle. The young fighter did not own an AAU card in his own name. Walker Smith Jr. had not progressed that far.

On that night, young Smith became Ray Robinson. Gainford had an extra AAU card with him assigned to a fighter of that name who had quit the team. Walker Smith Jr. made his amateur debut under the name Robinson and he kept it. It was like a show business switch, a studio shrinking the size of an ethnic name to make it easier to promote a star or simply for the public to pronounce. The name Walker Smith Jr. receded into the mists of trivia, remembered only by trivia experts.

Being 1-0 is better than starting 0-1, but it does not presage a brilliant career. Yet, Robinson was only growing into his skills. He embarked on a whirlwind pace of amateur fighting, dropping out of high school, fighting for whatever prizes were offered, most of them being merchandise. Robinson won so many watches, no one in his family would ever be caught unable to tell an inquirer the time.

Even if you were hawking watches on the equivalent of the black market during the Great Depression in the 1930s, there were not big bucks to be made. The adults in the church, impressed by Robinson, handed him dollar bills that he brought home to mom Leila to help feed the family.

In 1937, the Salem Crescent Athletic Club, by now starring Ray Robinson, journeyed to Watertown, New York, upstate some 60 miles north of Syracuse, to engage in a New York–Canada tournament. Jack Case, sports editor of the local *Watertown Daily Times*, became enamored with Robinson's talent and style.

Case was captivated by Robinson's performance, telling Gainford, "That's a sweet fighter you've got there, a real sweet fighter." A nearby observer added, "As sweet as sugar."[2] Although in his story, Case only wrote "Sugar Robinson," from then, the fighter acquired a lifetime nickname. This is how Robinson became Sugar Ray.

Robinson became a bigger hit the more people he hit. In 1939, he was the star of the Golden Gloves, even while he still weighed only 126 pounds. The event was conducted in front of 15,000 people in Madison Square Garden. Robinson was already known in the fight game before ever throwing a punch in the pros.

He was young and full of promise, and you didn't have to be Nat Fleischer, editor of *The Ring* magazine, to see it, though of course Fleischer did, too.

In late 1940, Robinson turned professional. His first of 200 pro fights took place on October 4 in Madison Square Garden where regular fight fans already knew him from his amateur success. The bout was on the undercard of the Henry Armstrong—Fritzie Zivic welterweight title fight. Robinson beat José Echevarria. Nonetheless, in his debut, Sugar Ray turned him into just another Joe, scoring a technical knockout at 51 seconds of the second round in a scheduled four-rounder. Being listed as Robinson's first opponent was the greatest fame Echevarria ever gained in the ring. He retired with a 3-38-5 record.

As self-assured as Robinson was by then, turning pro was no little thing, and years later he remembered well his thoughts that night in the dressing room before he climbed between the ropes.

"Rhythm is everything in boxing," Robinson said about the Echevarria fight. "Every move you make starts with your heart and that's in rhythm or you're in trouble. Your rhythm should set the pace of the fight. You make him fight your fight and that's what boxing's all about. In the dressing room that night, I could feel my rhythm beginning to move through me, and it assured me that everything would be all right." [3]

Robinson said Gainford told him not to be nervous, but Robinson claimed it was Gainford who was nervous.

"I was tingling now with excitement as I went up the wooden steps and bent to go through the ropes," Robinson said. [4]

Once he began throwing punches, Robinson understood that while Echevarria might have been a professional, other amateurs he had fought were equally as good. Robinson could beat him. And he did, rather handily. Robinson, showman that he was and, liking the noise of the crowd, talked of being disappointed that so many ringside seats were empty. The high rollers had not bothered to come early and were focused on the title fight. He intended to make them notice him in the future.

The march of Sugar Ray Robinson began there. He fought in New York, Georgia, and Philadelphia (several times). He jumped to six-rounders quickly. His first 10-rounder was in his thirteenth fight.

On July 31, 1941, Robinson beat Sammy Angott for the first time in a unanimous decision that lifted him to 21-0.

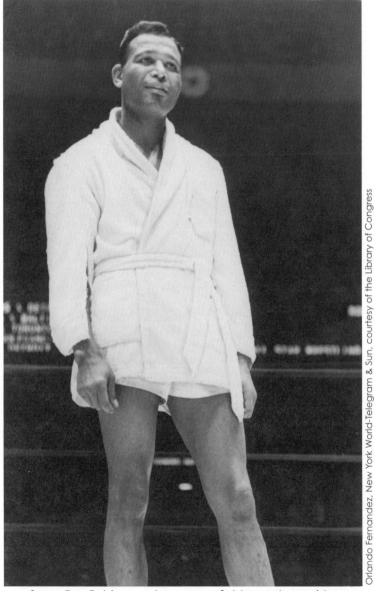

Orlando Fernandez, New York World-Telegram & Sun, courtesy of the Library of Congress

Sugar Ray Robinson, whom many fight experts consider the best boxer in history regardless of weight class, was Jake LaMotta's nemesis in the ring.

Angott was the reigning lightweight champ (135 pounds), but the belt was not at stake. Still, that was a major confidence booster.

In Robinson's twenty-sixth fight on October 31, 1941, he met Zivic for the first time and topped him by unanimous decision in 10 rounds at Madison Square Garden. Their return bout figured to be good box office given the closeness of the first encounter. The second one ended with Robinson winning again, this time by TKO at 31 seconds of the 10th round in a scheduled 12-round fight.

By the time Robinson fought LaMotta for the first time, he was a seasoned fighter.

It was against Jimmy Reeves in Cleveland that LaMotta first truly realized, beyond braggadocio, that he could be a very good fighter. He astonished his friend Pete Savage one day by bursting into tears. The reason?

"I'll never get big enough to fight Louis," he said. "If I get big enough so my weight will be anywhere near his, I'll be so fat and slow, he'll murder me." Accurate as the statement was, it was somewhat of a crazy one. LaMotta had been thinking and decided, "I could beat any man alive given the weight." [5]

Since Louis was a giant compared to him, LaMotta had to settle for tussling with Robinson. Robinson had pretty much cleaned out the welterweight division and LaMotta seemed like an intriguing matchup. LaMotta had a bigger name than other potential opponents.

It was a brave show and LaMotta went the distance. Robinson could hit him, but he could not put him down on the canvas. Robinson won a unanimous decision in front of 12,000 people at the Garden. Robinson's quickness was a difference maker. He ducked LaMotta's best shots.

"Robinson outpointed me over 10 rounds in the first fight, so I was down one," LaMotta said.[6]

Down one? Before the fight there was no hint there would ever be a second LaMotta–Robinson fight. But the result was an entertaining enough fight that it was only a matter of time before they met again. Together they could make more money than they could separately.

6

More Sugar Ray

If there was even a momentary thought that Jake LaMotta and Sugar Ray Robinson were done with one another in the ring after their first bout, it lasted only long enough for them to recover from the contact. The fight had been entertaining and the public liked what it saw. It was obvious to promoters, managers, trainers, and boxers that a rematch was logical and would be popular at the box office.

The first showdown was in the fall of 1942 and took place on the biggest indoor stage inside Madison Square Garden. Although Robinson won the bout, it was not one-sided. LaMotta gave a good accounting for himself. He was tough enough that he made believers out of skeptics.

Robinson was such an impressive fighter stylistically there was a body of opinion amongst many that he could not be beat. LaMotta did not beat him, but he made him look somewhat vulnerable. There were no fight fans running around saying, "Why would he fight him again?"

Less than a month after the match with Robinson, LaMotta returned to the ring. He was nothing if not active. He wasn't so rich he could take long vacations. Boxing was his job and after a sufficient interval, it was time to go back to work.

On the LaMotta opponent sheet, the foe he met on November 6, 1942, was called Henry Chmielewski. Chmielewski's given name when he was born in Poland was Henryk and he represented his country in the 1936 Summer Olympics in Berlin. He later moved to the United States to turn pro and sometimes fought under the name Henry Cheml.

LaMotta and Chmielewski met at the Mechanics Building in Boston where Jake won a unanimous decision. Keeping busy, LaMotta and Jimmy Edgar rumbled again at the Olympia in Detroit on New Year's Day in 1943. Edgar was just as difficult to get past this time as he had been in August 1942. LaMotta prevailed with a split decision.

Showing that he was almost always going to give fans a lengthy evening, LaMotta bested "California" Jackie Wilson on points at Madison Square Garden two weeks later. Merely a week after that, LaMotta recorded a rare stoppage, beating Charley Hayes on a technical knockout back at the Olympia. For a time, it seemed LaMotta was appearing at the Detroit venue as often as the hometown hockey team the Red Wings.

The win over Hayes was notable. He was a very solid fighter who had never been knocked down and his lifetime record was 29-8-1. LaMotta was his twelfth pro opponent and he was stopped in the sixth round.

All of this was prelude to another shot at Robinson, scheduled for February 5, 1943. LaMotta was keeping up a whirlwind pace. While he tended to gain weight between fights when he skirted training, trainer George Gainford was keeping him so active there was no time for breaks and no time to pile on excess poundage.

At this point, LaMotta was very motivated. He wanted another crack at Robinson. Jake was about as well-known and popular in Detroit as he was in New York, and Robinson had his early-life Detroit ties. LaMotta–Robinson II was scheduled for the Olympia.

Even if the two protagonists wanted to avoid one another, it would have been hard to do because of circumstances. World War II had drained the manpower of America, siphoning off the athletic and the hardy. Men were stuffed into uniforms, trained in a different way, and shipped overseas. There were not many credible and worthy opponents for either LaMotta or Robinson to fight if they didn't enter the ring together.

After the win over LaMotta, Robinson was hot after a title. While a rematch was always a prospect, he picked off a few more victories that were mere tune-ups. Robinson took out Izzy Jannazzo in Philadelphia, Victor Dellicurti (whom LaMotta had already visited with) in Madison Square Garden, Jannazzo again in Cleveland, and Al Nettlow in Philadelphia. These were not big money deals.

Robinson's record went to 36-0 after he beat LaMotta in 1942. *The Ring* magazine voted him Fighter of the Year for 1942. Robinson the showman wanted to please the crowd as well as win. But cleaning out the welterweight and middleweight divisions was one thing. He was not a world champion and felt he was more than ready to fight for a crown. LaMotta harbored the same thoughts.

The champion at 147 pounds, welterweight, was Red Cochrane who was awarded the title after beating Fritzie Zivic in 1941. In 1941, Billy Soose won the crown from Ken Overlin, but he never defended it, keeping the title in limbo before he retired during World War II.

Robinson wanted a shot at Cochrane, but his promoter, Mike Jacobs, informed him that he had heard very soon both Cochrane and Robinson were going to be drafted. If Robinson wanted to make some money first, he should sign to fight LaMotta (who it should be remembered was 4-F because of his ear troubles), which he did.

There was no time to take care of championship business for Robinson, but LaMotta meant business. Much later, Robinson confessed he spent much of his prep time for the bout pursuing women and staying out late and partying. At one point he wrote, "You left all your strength with those girls you were chasing." [1]

In a moment of reflection, Sugar Ray even recalled being uneasy in the ring just before the start of the bout when the contestants were being introduced. For a super confident athlete like him, it was a moment of uncomfortable reckoning never experienced before at this level of the sport. Robinson had always had swagger and knew he was going to win when he climbed between the ropes, but not this time.

As the Olympia crowd shouted during the introductions, Robinson thought, "Suddenly, for the first time in my boxing career, I was unsure of myself. That moment when you're being introduced, man, that's a boxer's moment of truth. You're all by yourself then. It's too late for anybody to help you, and what's worse it's too late for you to help yourself. That's what worried me." [2]

Robinson was right to be worried. LaMotta was more ready than Robinson, despite Robinson being a 3-1 favorite in the betting odds. His record had improved to 40-0. Most fight fans likely believed they would see a good match and bear witness to a good show, but if pushed to the wall most probably would have predicted Robinson was going to come out the winner. That's not what happened. It was LaMotta's night.

Jake did not score a knockout. He did not knock out a high percentage of foes and Robinson did not get knocked out often. Robinson, too, possessed a chin like a concrete wall. But LaMotta swarmed Robinson, kept him off-guard, and true to Sugar Ray's fears, he had blown his conditioning by not working hard enough in training and he felt it.

A pivotal moment occurred in the eighth round of the scheduled 10-rounder. LaMotta unloaded on Robinson and punched him through the ropes. A lesser man would have called it quits then, but Robinson lifted himself back through the ropes and back into contention. Still, it was a signature moment for LaMotta and he took the unanimous decision. It remains a famous result: LaMotta ending Robinson's winning streak.

"I would have to say that Robinson was the best I fought," LaMotta said. "A cutie, fast, with all the tricks. But he could also take a punch, and he could throw one." [3]

Robinson respected LaMotta, but he blamed himself for losing.

"When I walked out at the bell, Jake stomped me with his first left hook," Robinson said. "And he stomped me for ten rounds." Robinson viewed the eighth-round knockdown through the ropes this way: "He hit me with a right hand in my mid-section and when I doubled up, he let go a left hook to my jaw. For the first time in my career, I had no legs. I sagged through the ropes and onto the ring apron and sprawled there." [4]

Robinson was back on his feet by an eight count, but when the round ended, Gainford was snarling at him in the corner, reminding the fighter that he had been warned several times that he was not training properly.

Sugar Ray said he cried when the decision was announced, although it was no surprise to him. He was disheartened by his first loss, but also by a poor showing, and he felt embarrassed that he let down his friends in the crowd.

Perhaps more than any other athlete, a boxer enters the realm of competition with a belief in his own invincibility. Boxing is very personal. It is not a team sport. The other guy is out to get you, the swiftest way to victory being knocking your block off. Being scared is not an option, especially if you wish to win. The other guy often senses fear or doubt and capitalizes on it. Some boxers are never the same after they lose even once. Great fighters show what they are made of and they rebound.

By winning this bout from Robinson, LaMotta corrected mistakes he made in the first fight and proved what he felt was true in his own mind—that Robinson could be taken. It was a huge triumph for LaMotta. Not many men could defeat Sugar Ray Robinson when he was in his prime.

Robinson learned a lesson. He said he recalled fans booing as he sat on his stool in his corner after he lost.

"I made a vow never to get into a ring unless I was in perfect condition, unless I could face my moment of truth," Robinson said. That was something he should have already known, but Robinson's self-belief had crossed the line to cockiness against the wrong man.[5]

During this time, both Robinson and LaMotta were frustrated. Each believed that he was the best boxer in the world at his weight class. Each was being thwarted from even getting a shot at a title. LaMotta was road-blocked by gangsters. Robinson may or may not have been shunted aside because he was African American, but the war also played a role in limiting their opportunities, too. No governing body of the sport was going to strip a man for failure to defend the belt while he was serving his country during wartime. This meant there was a lot of paralysis in the sport. Joe Louis, the long-time heavyweight champ, was Exhibit A for this phenomenon. The title was frozen while he was in uniform overseas as a morale builder for the troops.

After being tipped about his impending induction into the Army, Robinson knew he was going to be short on income, at the very least, for some time. He could not predict the future or even know if he would be killed or injured in war. Hurriedly, another bout with LaMotta was arranged. Jake may have been staying on the home front, but he wasn't likely to get many big money chances for fights, either. Now that the men had each won once, this new fight, LaMotta–Robinson III, could be billed as a rubber match with winner claiming superiority.

Both fighters had followings in Detroit, so their third fight was again scheduled for the Olympia. It made sense and was a popular choice. The third fight was set for three weeks to the day after the second fight on February 26, 1943.

"My pride had prodded me into training hard this time," Robinson said.[6]

LaMotta was riding high after his win over Robinson. He said he received much more attention from sportswriters than ever before, was being talked about as the number one-ranked contender for the middleweight crown, and heard flattering words about his abilities more than ever before. Beating an undefeated Sugar Ray Robinson was no small thing.

Robinson was scheduled for Army induction the day after the bout. LaMotta groused about the way Sugar Ray was covered in the papers leading up to the third fight.

"I'm not knocking him on it," LaMotta said. "I would have done the same thing in his shoes, but he got every newspaper inch there was about the story of this brave boy off to fight for his country."[7]

The pattern for LaMotta–Robinson fights had already been established. Robinson was the guy on the move who could stay out of the way of big left hooks. LaMotta was the guy who took the fight to the other man. He was a swinger, while Robinson a jabber who bided his time.

This was another example of the fighters pretty much disregarding the weight limits of classes. At 160 ¾ pounds, LaMotta was a middleweight. At 145 pounds, Robinson was a welterweight. According to the *Associated Press* story about the fight, "Robinson was a one-man riot" in the early rounds[8]. He dominated Jake on points, something that would be telling later and overlooked by LaMotta in hindsight.

Robinson had LaMotta in trouble in the fourth round as he scored with both hands. However, in the seventh round, LaMotta trapped Robinson in his own corner and delivered a hard left hand to the face that dropped Sugar Ray to the canvas. Robinson took an eight count, but did not seem handicapped by the blow when the next round opened.

Referee Sam Hennessy's scorecard gave five rounds to Robinson and three to LaMotta. He scored 2 of the 10 rounds even. The two judges also saw it Robinson's way, though in close balloting, while the fans did not agree. They booed the result, apparently swayed by LaMotta's knockdown. LaMotta felt the same way. He believed he had done enough to capture the decision, pointing directly to the splashy knockdown. But that would only have won him one round on a round-scoring system. On a 10-point-must system, he could have won the round 10-8.

"I didn't lose it, he got the decision," LaMotta said. "That's when I began to think of Robinson as a nemesis."[9]

A day later, Robinson became a member of the U.S. Army and was given the rank of private.

It would be two years before the two men who defined boxing's two middle weight classes met again in the ring. Many major developments would affect both their individual lives and the future of the United States before that occurred.

In theory, Robinson went off to war, but he did not engage in combat. LaMotta stayed at home and engaged in more battles than anyone knew about for a long time.

7

Vikki LaMotta

It's hard to know what it meant when Jake LaMotta wrote his autobiography, *Raging Bull,* and he spelled the first name of his second wife incorrectly throughout. Her name was not "Vickie," but "Vikki," as she emphatically pointed out years later.

At the time of his death in 2017, Jake LaMotta had been married seven times, but through his actions and statements, it seems obvious that the true love of his life was Vikki. At various times, other wives would become jealous of Vikki. She was the featured woman in Jake's life in *Raging Bull,* and she was an advisor to principals on the film of the same name when they subsequently brought Jake's story to a wider audience.

The woman born Beverly Rosalyn Thailer in the Bronx in 1930 married the boxer when she was 16 years old. Her stunning good looks matched the beauty of Hollywood actresses, and she in all ways resembled the type referred to as a blonde bombshell in the capital of movie making.

Raging Bull was dramatic enough in dissecting LaMotta's life as he made his way through the boxing world to claim the middleweight championship of the world. However, the sub-plot of his life with Vikki (and that covered only a tiny part of their time together and veered away from their future years) could have been a mini-series all by its lonesome.

LaMotta was neither a gentleman nor a guy most girls would bring home to Momma. He could show a sweet side when courting, but after time passed, after the marriage became legal, and he began living in close quarters every day, by his own admission he could be a pig to women.

There is no other way to summarize it. In the past, LaMotta may have gotten away with his verbally and physically abusive ways. In this modern era, wives would more likely have had him arrested, hauled into court, and locked up for some of the treatment he afforded them. LaMotta was as jealous as any man who ever walked the earth, and destructively so. Under the influence of alcohol and intense fury, LaMotta was liable to say or do something that harmed people he professed to love.

LaMotta pretty much damned himself in his own 20-20 hindsight of years spent with Vikki—an uncomfortable-to-read, baring-of the-soul in his autobiography. More damning, many years later, Vikki wrote her own autobiography with respected boxing writer Thomas Hauser. After she finished it, she chose to shelve the whole story to be held until after her death. That book, called *Knockout: The Sexy, Violent, Extraordinary Life of Vikki LaMotta* appeared in print in 2006, a year after her death at age 75, and 20 years after it was completed.

For all his passion and love for Vikki, LaMotta did not seem to know how to have a long-term constructive relationship with her or any woman. What LaMotta could do when he first met a woman he liked was turn on the charm, but he could never sustain it in a personal relationship. However, later in life he was able to charm audiences on a nightly basis to make a buck in his nightclub act. Much of his treatment of his multiple wives would be vilified today, but there was much less societal focus on domestic abuse when LaMotta was younger. Such organizations as the National Coalitions Against Domestic Violence, Women Against Abuse, and the Battered Women Justice Project came into existence later to aid women like Vikki LaMotta and Jake LaMotta's other wives.

Jake's personal life was always a bit erratic. LaMotta was married when he met Vikki. He married a Bronx woman named Ida, who was 19 when LaMotta was 20 in 1941. They had a child, a girl named Jacklyn, together, but parenthood did not keep them together. LaMotta said the reality was they were too young and immature to marry and probably never should have wedded.

"To be honest about it, the thing that got us together was plain sex," he said. "She had a great body and I was crazy for her. It was a marriage that was fated to break up, which it did about a year later." [1]

In the book Raging Bull, LaMotta summarized his married lives (plural) by saying, "My basic trouble was that I got married more than I should, not that I'm saying anything against any of my wives. Why the hell should I? After all, St. Peter ain't ever going to give me his personal regards. I'm no bargain." [2]

For a man who much of his life seemed insecure in his relationships with women, that was candid self-analysis.

LaMotta even admitted being "nuts back then" [3] during this general period. He drunk himself so stupid at one of his own parties he basically knocked himself out. When he awoke, only a few people remained in his apartment, but Ida was lying unconscious on the floor. Brother Joey informed the memory-shortchanged Jake that he had punched her out because he thought she was flirting with another woman. Joey told Jake that all attempts to rouse her had failed and he thought she was dead.

Sluggishly clueing into the situation, LaMotta envisioned going to jail. He called his friend Pete Savage, a small-time criminal at the time, and asked for advice. While LaMotta was waiting on Pete's arrival, Joey suggested disposing of the body in the river (unspecified, but probably the East River). Jake gave serious consideration to this.

Looking back, LaMotta expressed no remorse about belting his wife, knocking her out cold, or possibly killing her. He only worried how her violent death might impact his career. "Right now," he said years later, "it sounds like I was a maniac to be even thinking of throwing a woman in the river, but maybe I was a maniac back then." [4]

Pete, who was sober, suggested calling a doctor to check out his wife might be a good idea and Jake agreed. Turns out, she was not dead, merely out of it.

"But it was a marriage that was headed for divorce from the start," LaMotta said. "The kind of dame who would marry a guy like me was slated to end up divorced." [5]

Apparently, LaMotta forgot that thought when he moved on to Vikki as his second wife.

Simply pouring over the words of the couple's accounts of their time spent together can make a reader cringe. They resemble the script of a reality TV show at its worst.

In her story, Vikki LaMotta tells of being born to a father, Abraham, whose immigrant side of the family were Jews from Romania, and to a mother, Margaret Ruth, from Poughkeepsie, New York. She said her family was poor, but her father only worked odd jobs and gambled at cards. He usually left the family with $1 for food and invested the rest of his gambling earnings in more gambling. If Vikki believed in Santa Claus as a child, the illusion evaporated quickly.

Wearing shoes with holes in them and clothes that were ragged, at age eight or nine, she took on odd jobs in New York City, tucking her then-brown hair under a cap and masquerading as a boy to shine shoes. Young Vikki possessed an insatiable curiosity. She said she was mostly a happy child despite the hardships and loved people watching in the streets, constantly peppering workers with questions about their jobs.

In a rather unusual development, at eight years old, Vikki began hanging around a collection of cab drivers just to listen to their stories. They got used to her and eventually she began riding around with them on their calls. She saw different neighborhoods, including the fancier ones of New York City. One taxi driver named Willie Goldberg took a particular interest in Vikki's welfare, bought her ice cream, took her to the movies (unheard of pleasures in the Thailer family), and even gave her a jacket. They became what she called close friends.

Vikki's best friends in high school were Puerto Rican, and one day, fooling around, they decided they would all change their first names as a lark. That's how the youngster born Beverly became Vikki. The name Vikki stuck to her for the rest of her life.

In high school, Vikki thought she was coming into her own a little bit. She was sexually unaware, not terribly focused on her looks, but she was a looker who drew stares for being beautiful. Her friends wanted to go out at night and go to dances. Her father was overly strict and wanted her home early. She defied him and stayed out late. To her shock, Vikki's father began beating her when she ignored her curfew.

This disgraceful series of episodes began when she returned home 10 minutes late once and was grounded for two weeks. She paid no attention to the punishment and went to a dance anyway.

"And when I got home, my father was waiting, beside himself with rage," she said. "He had never hit me before; maybe a spanking when I was little. This time he walked toward me without a word, raised his fists and hit me. And then he kept hitting me. That's what a beating is. It's not a flash explosion or one punch in anger. It's sustained punishment. He punched me. I moved away. He'd catch up and punch me again. I couldn't believe it was happening. This was my father!" [6]

Vikki's mother never intervened or aided her daughter.

This sickening series of events continued for about a year, in Vikki LaMotta's recollection. She kept on going out with her friends. Sometimes she was later getting home than the deadline was decreed, whether due to spending a little too much time with friends or irregular running subway trains. The Thailers had no telephone, so she could not call. Eventually, and sadly, she determined this was the cost of doing business. The old man was going to punch her out when she came home, so she might as well stay out as long as she felt like it.

She estimated her father beat her about a dozen times during that period. After a while, when she was going to school with bruises on her face, she said he changed tactics, switching to a rubber hose. Vikki said she took the hits stoically and refused to cry to show she could not be beaten down. One time, he declared he was going to hit her until she did cry. On another occasion, he kicked her while wearing heavy boots.

After one of those dances when she thought she was getting a ride home, Vikki said she was raped by a thug and lost her virginity. She lamented not reporting him to the police, but said later this guy was murdered.

When Vikki was 15 years old, her father cut all her hair off as a different form of punishment. It was then that she dyed the stubble of her hair blonde and stayed with that color for the rest of her life. That was the last time her father abused her.

Such abusive treatment must leave scars on the psyche, but Vikki LaMotta did not seem to dwell as much on these beatings' impact on her as she might have.

Looking much older than her age, also at 15, Vikki took a job as a dancer at a nightclub (not a stripper) and was thrilled to be making $20 a night, totaling $100 a week.

That same year, Vikki was at the beach one day with friends when someone passed around the program from a boxing card. They all leafed through the pages and she was struck by a photo of a young fighter. It was Jake LaMotta.

The next year the Thailer family somehow scraped together money for a pool membership. One day a young man approached her. It was Joey LaMotta, Jake's younger brother, who said he recognized immediately Vikki was Jake's type. He told her so, too.

"He'd really flip," Joey said.[7]

The next day Joey introduced Vikki to Jake. Jake in the flesh had the same impact on Vikki as Jake in the program photograph had.

"Soft eyes," she said. "Shy and laid back. There was nothing pretentious or brazen about him."[8]

Jake LaMotta felt a tingle when he met Vikki, too.

"When I met Vikki, it was love at first sight," he said. "She was so pretty, just a baby. And I said to myself, 'That's mine. She belongs to me.'"[9]

Years later, Vikki commented on Jake's statement, having accumulated more up-close-and-personal knowledge about him.

"That was Jake, talking about the day we met," she said. "Possessive, wasn't he?"[10]

Young Jake LaMotta and Vikki, who would become his second wife, met at a community pool in the Bronx.

Acme News Photos

If that even crossed her mind as a teenager, it was unlikely. What did cross her mind was being told that Jake was married. There already was a Mrs. LaMotta. She was on the way out the door, though, whether she knew it or not yet. Vikki said she was not interested in dating married men, so it was convenient that Jake was about to get divorced.

In between clobbering Ida and divorcing her and starting to date Vikki (although the exact timing was not specified by LaMotta in his book), Jake was guilty of egregious and monstrous behavior with a female acquaintance from the neighborhood who was a good friend of his pal Pete.

Pete had been sent to prison for some of his misdemeanors and Jake said he would watch out for her.

This woman, Viola, told Jake that Pete asked her to ask Jake to write to him in prison. LaMotta told her he was incapable of writing a letter and said he had never written one in his life. However, he could dictate his thoughts to her. He told her that he would come over her house in 20 minutes for the task, figuring he would produce a few sentences. Viola was younger than Pete and Jake, but had grown up. She had a date that night, and when LaMotta arrived at her home for the letter-writing assignment, she was dressed up. Jake, who had previously dismissed her as a kid, now thought she looked very sexy.

Viola had never liked LaMotta and at times essentially told him she thought he was a creep. LaMotta had never thought much of her either, but suddenly he was aroused by her appearance. Very quickly things escalated. LaMotta admitted he grabbed her, kissed her, and even as she cried and fought him he raped her. All the while he was telling her that he and Pete were best friends and shared girls. Only, it turned out Viola was not that kind of girl at all. He told her he didn't believe her when she told him she was a virgin, but only realized it too late.[11]

LaMotta was fortunate he didn't go to prison, but there was no case made against him. Only much later did he mention Viola became a different person after his violence. Reading between the lines about Viola's future life, there are hints LaMotta may have ruined her life because of his assault. That shameful episode was a one-night interlude around the time of the disappearance of Ida from LaMotta's life and his courtship of Vikki.

Vikki liked the romance and the excitement of being squired around by a pro fighter. She got pregnant before Jake was divorced from Ida. She did not tell LaMotta right away. She thought about an abortion, but considered that a sin. When she told Jake she was pregnant, though, he became excited about the prospect of having a son. Jake put a lawyer on his divorce case with Ida, and it was done in Mexico. Then he told Vikki they were getting married.

For a while in the early stages of their relationship, Vikki was swept away by the glamour of being romanced by a major sports figure. That spell was already waning, however. Reminding herself she was only 16 and did not want to get tied down, Vikki panicked about getting married. On the day of their wedding, Vikki was shaking with fear and remorse. She retreated to a bathroom and began crying and throwing up. This was going to be a small wedding, with only parents from her side of the family. Sensing her daughter's dismay, this time mom stepped up and told Vikki she could still call things off if she didn't want to get married. But Vikki thought the advice came too late and she went through with the ceremony.

After marrying in 1946, Vikki and Jake had three children together, one daughter and two sons. Their marriage lasted 11 years until 1957, and some of it was hell for Vikki, who basically transformed from a wide-eyed teenager to a mature mother devoted to her kids.

Jake worshipped Vikki. He was amazed such a beautiful woman would fall for him. But he didn't take long after they had married to exert his usual crass style in bossing her around, controlling her movements, and exhibiting jealousy towards almost anyone she spent any time with, male or female.

Concurrent with this, LaMotta's boxing career was stymied by the mob. He kept winning bouts, but he wasn't getting any closer to a title shot. To LaMotta's credit, he would not play along with the mob, would not buckle to gangsters' authority and turn his career over to their management. In retaliation, after several overtures were made and rejected by LaMotta, the big boys made sure LaMotta could not get a sniff of the middleweight crown. He toiled for fight after fight. He built a major fan following. But he wasn't going to get the big prize without cooperating with the mobsters or getting their blessing.

One day, Pete Savage, salvaged from prison, was visiting the LaMottas. Savage asked Jake why he had not yet received a shot at the title. Vikki, who had been making sandwiches in the other room, brought them in while they were talking and answered the question for LaMotta.

"Because he thinks he's so smart, that's why," Jake quoted Vikki as saying in his book. "He could have been the champ for the last three years, but he knows more than anybody else. He isn't going to play ball with anybody, he isn't." [12]

Vikki was young and may have been naïve about what was really going on. She may not have appreciated at that age that Jake was resisting being anyone's puppet. Perhaps she couldn't see through the fog. Not that Jake clearly explained the stark situation.

"Aw, shaddup!" Jake retorted. "I told you to keep your mouth shut about that. Just like every broad, shootin' your mouth off. Well, shoot it off about something else besides my business." LaMotta directed that verbal assault at Vikki. When speaking of the conversation later, he added, "That's a wife for you, drilling the old needle into the same old spot in that same sore tooth, even though she knew how goddamned mad it always made me." [13]

Jake was getting meaner, but he had not been quite that romantic even on their wedding night. That night she said, when she retreated to Jake's apartment, she saw some of Ida's clothes still in the closet and said it felt as if she was moving into a home where the other woman had died.

After they made love on their wedding night, Vikki said she turned to the wall and cried. Even then, almost immediately, she felt trapped by what she had committed to doing and being.

8

Still Title Dreaming

For all their crowd-pleasing mini-wars in the ring, as Sugar Ray Robinson went off to U.S. Army service in Europe, mostly entertaining troops, neither he nor Jake LaMotta owned the middleweight championship belt. Robinson had beaten Jake two out of three times, although each fight was close. Now with Robinson out of the picture, LaMotta had to find new opponents, or other repeat opponents, to stay active on the home front.

He was no closer to a shot at fulfilling his dream of winning the 160-pound championship. Fight fans loved him, and boxing experts admired him. The guys that controlled the sport behind the scenes despised him and only grew angrier with him the more frequently he deflected attempts by the mob to control his career. However, the gangsters in essence *were* controlling LaMotta's career. He was willing to fight anyone anywhere, and they didn't care as long as he did not fight the holder of the belt.

This was the long-running soap opera of LaMotta's professional life. But once Robinson went into the Army, LaMotta faced an even more limited field of opponents who could provide a good match and help bring in the people.

Only weeks after Robinson became an enlisted man, LaMotta returned to the ring to face Jimmy Reeves again. They had met twice before in the fall of 1941. It was a respectable match, the kind a matchmaker can promote under the guise of LaMotta seeking revenge. Reeves bested LaMotta by split decision and unanimous decision. Yet now LaMotta's reputation had been enhanced, so even if he was 0-2 in the series he seemed more likely this time around to claim a win.

The men met for a third time in the Olympia in Detroit, very much a home away from home for LaMotta, on March 19, 1943. This time Jake prevailed. LaMotta knocked Reeves out in the sixth round and said he was paid $6,000 for the work, "which is a thousand dollars a round. I was fighting good," LaMotta said. "I made more than a million dollars in purses [through his career] and you don't win that by fighting your Aunt Sadie." [1]

A couple of fights later in May, LaMotta commenced a new rivalry. His new opponent was Fritzie Zivic. Zivic, born in 1913, was of Croatian extraction, and, although he was born in Pittsburgh, his nickname was "The Croat Comet." Zivic was one of five brothers, all of whom fought. Collectively, they were known as "The Fighting Zivics."

In 1940, Zivic won the world welterweight title, at 147 pounds, in an upset 15-round decision over Henry Armstrong, who gained lasting fame for winning championships in three of the eight weight classes. Zivic claimed that Armstrong fought dirty, elbowing him and the like, and he only began to catch up in the later rounds when he did likewise. The fight ended with Zivic knocking Armstrong down just before the final bell.

Zivic's given name was Ferdinand Henry John Zivcich. He was a bold and determined fighter, and like LaMotta, he was prepared to fight anyone available. He was always ready to rumble. During his lengthy pro career, Zivic fought a remarkable 232 times, compiling a record of 158-64-9 with one no contest. He was a bit more of a knockout puncher than LaMotta, collecting 80 KOs.

LaMotta and Zivic went after each other for the first time on June 10, 1943, in Forbes Field, home of the Pittsburgh Pirates and basically Zivic's home field. Even before the first time the duo met, *The Ring* magazine saw the possibilities in such a showdown. A story in the April 1943 issue praised both Zivic and LaMotta for their impressive fights with Beau Jack and Sugar Ray Robinson, respectively. *The Ring* also took note of sellout crowds attending those two major bouts. This story may well be where the idea was hatched of putting them together in the ring.

The Armstrong fight notwithstanding, Zivic developed a reputation for dirty fighting. Once labeled a dirty fighter, Zivic could not shed the impression. "Every time Zivic entered the ring he was booed and hissed because of his ring tactics that are not exactly according to Hoyle," *The Ring* article stated.[2]

However, the fans came around to Zivic. They began seeing him as a warrior, and he evolved from a pariah into a fan favorite. He also did so seemingly without first cleaning up his act. Perhaps Zivic had become more clever or subtle in his ways. He did receive his share of foul calls, but mostly he provided a good action show.

As anticipated, LaMotta–Zivic was a good fight. It was also close, with Jake winning a split decision in Zivic's hometown. On July 12, 1943, they fought again at Forbes Field, and this time Zivic walked off with the win by split decision.

"He was one of the roughest little customers that ever put on gloves," LaMotta said of Zivic.[3]

Jake did not really think Zivic beat him in their second bout. He quoted a headline in a local newspaper commenting on the result. It read, "LaMotta Wins, Zivic Gets Nod."[4]

LaMotta and Zivic then took a break from one another's company, each owning one victory over the other. Jake scored wins over Ossie Harris and Tony Ferrara. They padded his résumé a bit, but any fight that did not get him a shot at the title was just killing time. LaMotta could not make that much money fighting guys nobody heard of, and there was no budging on his overall place in the universe. The mob owned the title and had LaMotta on a string. All he could do was keep fighting, and keep finding opponents to fill his dance card.

"The months passed and even the years," LaMotta said.[5]

LaMotta had zero chance at the title even though he was the number-one-ranked contender in the middleweight division for a couple of years. Still, nobody was knocking on his door, and he was frustrated at being stymied just short of his dream.

Zivic was the most credible foe out there, and it wasn't long before the camps of the two fighters realized it. If they met again, they would sell out the arena and obtain the biggest payday available. A third LaMotta–Zivic bout took place on November 12, 1943. This time the encounter shifted to LaMotta's home turf of Madison Square Garden. The bout was as intense and action-packed as the first two meetings. LaMotta won by a split decision.

One might think LaMotta and Zivic were sick of one each other. But no, they signed to fight for a fourth time on January 14, 1944. The LaMotta–Zivic rivalry was taking on overtones of LaMotta–Robinson. It didn't quite energize the public to the same degree, but when they did meet, fans wanted to see it. LaMotta-Zivic was good at the box office, and putting the fighters together made for good paydays.

LaMotta edged Zivic in their fourth bout, scoring a unanimous decision at the Olympia in Detroit. LaMotta fought in Detroit so often during the early 1940s, it was as if he was a native. He certainly built a following there out of familiarity.

The 4-F LaMotta was gold in 1943 at the height of the war. During that era, fighters fought. Jake fought 13 times in 1943, and, by his own mathematical reckoning, he made six figures.

"That was the year, 1943, that I earned over a hundred thousand dollars, which is not bad for a ninth-grade drop-out from the Bronx slums," he said.[6]

That didn't count the fourth Zivic fight, which took place just two weeks into the next year. However, LaMotta noted again and again despite being both busy and successful in the ring, nobody was calling to offer him a shot at the middleweight title. He was still frozen out and frustrated by his circumstances. This treatment went on for years. LaMotta was being waited out through his prime by the gangsters who remained in charge of the sport.

Patience did not come naturally to LaMotta. There was only one course of action to follow in his mind, and he was following it. Keep on fighting and keep on winning. Friend Pete Savage counseled the same. LaMotta hoped he would build up such a record that all the sportswriters would rally to his cause, write about his performances, and talk about how he deserved his chance to fight for the crown. He hoped the pressure would build and his opponents outside the ring would yield.

Whether that was a naïve position or not, at the least it was noble. LaMotta refused to sell out. He wanted to make it to the top through his own efforts, unaided by anyone, and especially wished to resist allowing anyone else to take control of his career.

LaMotta pressed on. He fought and beat Ossie Harris twice in the first two months of 1944. A Pittsburgh guy like Zivic, Harris was what was often referred to in boxing as a war horse. Harris would give an honest day's work, but he was not so talented he was a threat to beat the best fighters. His lifetime record was 45-51-5. Harris's nickname was "Bulldog," apparently because he tenaciously kept on coming.

Harris also fought Zivic three times. After losing the first two, Harris prevailed in the third bout. He fought the esteemed Tony Zale, too, but lost. Harris definitely did not duck the best guys around. He gave a strong accounting of himself against LaMotta both times in 1944, split decisions twice favoring Jake.

LaMotta also polished off Coley Welch (92-20-5 lifetime), Lou Woods (44-10), Lloyd Marshall (70-25-4), and George Kochan (40-22-11) twice. They weren't headliners, but they were all respectable fighters who had a puncher's chance against LaMotta.

Then along came Sugar Ray Robinson again as the calendar turned once more. Robinson got out of the Army early through a strange development. Unlike Joe Louis, who genuinely seemed to like the service he was performing, Robinson despised the Army. To him it was like watching an hourglass track the lost time in his career. Above all, he hated being a nobody at southern military bases, where he felt discrimination. Robinson had never faced such racist treatment and did not tolerate it well. He easily could have blown a gasket, punched out a white soldier taunting him, been sent to the brig, and given a court martial.

Robinson was in an alien environment much of the time, and he did not want to put up with it any longer. In Harlem, Robinson was a king. He drove a pink Cadillac, drank champagne, had a devoted following, and was a star and celebrity to a degree few other African Americans had experienced up to that point in American history. It was no secret Robinson wanted out, but how could he neatly and justifiably escape his Army predicament? Robinson went into the Army in 1943, but was back in New York before the end of 1944. How did he end up back in civilian garb so quickly?

On March 29, after a poker game involving Joe Louis ended with a Robinson loss of a big hand while holding four jacks, Robinson stood up and left the card game. Fellow soldiers at first thought he was blowing off steam and hadn't gone far from the game. But, in reality, Robinson had walked off the post, out of Fort Hamilton in Brooklyn, New York, and was nowhere to be seen at roll call the next morning. Robinson vanished and the Army was upset and concerned. Sugar Ray was working in public relations for them. But, where was he? Officials did not really want to arrest a popular celebrity troop morale builder. It took six days to find Robinson, who turned up in a hospital in Staten Island. He informed Army officials that he had suffered amnesia in a fall after hitting his head which medical personnel confirmed.

This sounded too unbelievable to be true, especially on the eve of a scheduled departure for Robinson to entertain troops in Europe (something which he had groused about doing). To say Army superiors were skeptical was putting it mildly, but all investigation into his whereabouts (he was found wandering the street in New York City) and his health could not disprove Robinson's story.

The hospital medical report read, in part, "He was unable to give any information about his past life or the events leading up to his hospitalization and he failed to recognize relatives who visited him."[7] It sounded like a fairy tale to suspicious Army authorities.

In the end, as Robinson reported suffering from constant headaches, he missed his assignment to Europe while recuperating on Staten Island. Ultimately, the Army gave Robinson an honorable discharge on June 3, 1944.

Amnesia? Hardly anyone knew what to think about that. Of course, as soon as he was able, Robinson returned to the fight game. He was on his own by early June and fought for pay again on October 27, beating Lou Woods. Robinson swiftly regained his form and won six more fights in a row. He seemed to remember all his old moves. When Robinson was sharp again, who was waiting? Naturally, Jake LaMotta. Why not fight for a fourth time?

They signed to meet on February 23, 1945. Almost exactly two years had passed since their last meeting on the eve of Robinson's induction into the Army. Only shortly before, LaMotta had recorded his first victory in the series. It was still the only loss on Robinson's record.

Robinson had been away from the ring and knew he had to be ready for LaMotta, a determined foe who would not drop to the canvas regardless of what Robinson threw at him. Robinson would never take LaMotta lightly again. The war in Europe and Japan still raged, but LaMotta and Robinson were renewing hostilities. Facing LaMotta once more was one way for Robinson to test his fitness.

LaMotta also knew what was in store. He had seen enough of Robinson in three prior fights to understand his style and moves. He had proven to himself that yes, he could take Robinson. LaMotta might have been buoyed by figuring he was the victor most recently, and that Robinson might show some ring rust despite his busy renewal schedule.

Robinson was taking some public grief for his peculiar departure from the Army, and Army leaders were wondering about his seemingly swift and complete recovery from those headaches. Despite those mysterious head problems, he was somehow boxing again and winning all his fights.

For all the negative publicity and all the time that had passed since the previous bout between the two men, fight fans craved another opportunity to see LaMotta and Robinson square off again. More than 18,000 turned out, standing room only in early 1945 at Madison Square Garden. This fight resembled the previous ones in several ways. Robinson, known for his dapper style in and out of the ring, may have surprised Jake by taking the fight to him. Forcing the action, Robinson cut LaMotta on the forehead in the first round. In the third round, a Robinson left cut LaMotta's lip.

Some felt LaMotta was beaten, almost out on his feet, but in the sixth round, the bull was more combative, targeting Robinson with numerous good shots. Suddenly, LaMotta shifted the momentum of the fight in his favor. Briefly, it seemed a LaMotta knockout of Robinson was possible. But Sugar Ray rallied, directing the bout away from the ropes and back into the center of the ring, and pounded away at LaMotta anew.

At the end, both men were standing, though LaMotta seemed exhausted. They had given their all and the fight went the 10-round distance. Robinson claimed a unanimous decision (the scorekeepers had an easy time of it, giving Sugar Ray six or seven rounds each), and he led LaMotta 3-1.

At that time, they may have thought they would never fight again, although they may have believed that one day they were destined to meet in a title bout, as at that time neither Sugar Ray Robinson nor Jake LaMotta owned a title.

This was such a rousing fight that, again, people wanted to see more. It seemed the paying boxing customer never tired of the LaMotta–Robinson punch-outs. Even though Robinson ended up winning most of the time, there was always an overriding sense that something surprising could happen like a LaMotta haymaker connecting and knocking out Robinson. Who knew? Even if that never happened, buying tickets for their matches was a good investment because there was always enough action to make the cost worthwhile.

Four times was not enough, so Robinson and LaMotta agreed to go at it again, seven months later, on September 17, 1945.

In between, Robinson tussled with such pros as George Costner (74-12-3 lifetime) whom he knocked out in one round, and Jose Basora (78-20-7), with whom he drew. Outside of LaMotta, Basora was the first man Robinson fought whom he did not beat.

One of the guys LaMotta topped between the fourth and fifth fights with Robinson was Basora. He beat him by TKO. LaMotta also knocked out Costner in six rounds. For those looking for clues as to how Jake would fare this time against Robinson, those two comparative results may be encouraging or not. Given that this was LaMotta–Robinson, such details probably didn't matter anyway.

The fight was scheduled for 12 rounds, a first for both men, and the venue was Chicago's Comiskey Park. It was the home of the Chicago White Sox, a stadium that could hold many more people than Olympia or Madison Square Garden.

Robinson was not going to catch LaMotta by surprise by pressuring him from the start. LaMotta learned his lesson in the fourth fight. He was known for such tactics, and he came out employing his traditional style. Robinson was a master of the left jab, but for the first few rounds LaMotta brushed off that normally effective weapon. It took a while, but Robinson finally caught up to Jake.

Sugar Ray, like a future Muhammad Ali, had the kind of coordination and speed, while being light on his feet, which enabled him to score points with punches while he was moving away from an opponent. That strategy affected LaMotta, and he did not know how to counter it. Still, whatever Robinson did, LaMotta weathered it. Whatever LaMotta threw at Robinson, he endured. However, in the last minute of the fight, the end of the 12th round, Robinson staggered LaMotta with a big left-right combination.

LaMotta, as he proudly pointed out each time a Robinson fight concluded, managed to stay on his feet. Robinson was given a split decision by the judges. He owned four victories over LaMotta in five tries, but almost all of them by scant scoring margins.

"LaMotta is the toughest man I have ever fought," Robinson said after that bout.[8]

He just couldn't understand how LaMotta could absorb so much punishment and fail to go down. They had been through 52 rounds of ferocious boxing together and not once had the great Sugar Ray Robinson been able to propel Jake LaMotta to the canvas.

They were both wildly popular sports figures. They had engaged in one of the toughest rivalries in all of sport, but as the end of 1945 neared, neither Robinson nor LaMotta had been given a single chance to fight for a world title.

"The only thing I really wanted was that title," LaMotta said.[9]

9

The Fix

Gangsters never left Jake alone. Sometimes they would take aside his brother, Joey, and let him know that if LaMotta cooperated with them he would get a shot at the middleweight title. Sometimes the mobsters talked to Jake's best friend, Pete Savage, and asked him to deliver the same message. Occasionally, they would summon Jake himself to a meeting and tell him the same thing. He would spurn them, walk out on them, and pretty much insult them. There were often veiled threats about LaMotta's well-being. He was told that he may be famous as a highly ranked boxer, known far and wide, but he was still not bigger than they were.

These types of scenarios played out repeatedly over the years. LaMotta was a hot commodity in the boxing world, but he was no closer to fighting for the title in 1947 than he had been in 1943. He was working against the inevitable with time eroding his skills while all the bad guys had to do was sit and wait. They allowed LaMotta the freedom to fight whoever he pleased as long as the bout was not for the crown. Jake annoyed them, irritated them, and bugged them, but rather than break his arm or leg or worse, they always let him walk away because he could not walk far. LaMotta was cornered. He despised being incarcerated at Coxsackie, but the reality was that his circumstances now were not so very different. There were always walls erected around him.

The thing Jake LaMotta wanted most in life was to be recognized as the best middleweight fighter in the world. It defined his being. And he could not even get a chance to win the championship. Many boxers start out believing they can be the best. Most are disappointed somewhere along the way and must live with the disappointment that they were not as good as they thought they were. LaMotta had to live with the frustration of being denied the chance to prove he was the best. The phrase "uncrowned" champion is bandied around a lot in boxing. It comes up when boxing fans and sportswriters realize the best fighter in a certain weight class is not the man holding the belt. Such recognition only goes so far, though. Another popular phrase is, "You could look it up." Well, you can't look it up if the topic is an uncrowned champion. You've got to put your name in the books so that anyone can look it up for all time.

In old age, a denied Jake LaMotta might be asked by a grandchild, "Did you ever win the championship?" Or, "Did you ever fight for the title?" He wanted the answer to be "Yes," not a long-winded explanation about why it was "No."

Of course, LaMotta was not the only boxer whose career was affected by crooks that controlled the fight game during his prime. Some fighters had their entire careers directed by people pulling strings, built up in the public eye and for sportswriters with a long list of victories against opponents where the results were fixed in their favor.

The most prominent example of a big-name fighter having his career controlled by gangsters was heavyweight Primo Carnera, the Italian import nicknamed "The Ambling Alp." Carnera was gargantuan in size but of limited talent. Yet, he was guided carefully past more dangerous fighters. Peculiar things kept occurring in his bouts, but he always ended up on top. Carnera was eventually exposed by Max Baer when the mobsters washed their hands of him. Baer knocked Carnera down 11 times as the crown changed hands.

LaMotta was not looking for breaks. He was not looking for a lineup of boxers he could polish off. He was fearless. Jake took on anyone willing to stand in front of him. He had reached the position of top contender on his own merit, building a reputation of credibility with fans in New York, Detroit, Cleveland, and in any city where he appeared. He wasn't even limited to just 160-pounders in the middleweight class. He fought light heavies of 175, too. LaMotta was tough-looking and rugged in the ring, even if he was not that large. But it didn't matter to him if he gave away weight.

By 1947, LaMotta was at a stage where all he wanted out of his career was for people outside the ring to get out of his way and let him take care of business. However, he was road-blocked.

Then along came Billy Fox. Under normal circumstances, LaMotta would have been happy to fight Fox in a phone booth or baseball stadium, under a big top tent or on the boardwalk in Atlantic City. But the gangsters had a special interest in Fox's career. It was said that behind the scenes Fox's career was directed by Philadelphia crime boss Frank "Blinky" Palermo, and Palermo wanted Fox to keep on winning.

Fox, whose nickname was "Blackjack," was a pretty good fighter on paper who in 58 career bouts ended up 48-9-1. He won the first 36 of his fights before talk began of matching him against LaMotta. By then, Fox had already challenged for the light-heavyweight title, but was knocked out by Gus Lesnevich. After that loss in February 1947, Fox won six more times.

It finally reached a point in negotiations with the mob (if they could be called negotiations rather than ultimatums) where LaMotta was worn down. He was offered a chance to fight Fox—and guarantee a loss, a fixed result—which would then guarantee him his long-awaited title shot. Initially, LaMotta was offered $100,000 to accept the loss to Fox, but he turned down the bucks. He said all he wanted in return was a chance at the middleweight title.

LaMotta had stood up for his principles for four years and despite his high-profile series of fights with Sugar Ray Robinson and his victories over just about everyone else, he was no closer to a championship.

"What was I going to do, fight the mob for the rest of my life?" LaMotta asked himself. "This was the establishment. What they say went. I'd been fighting them now for four years and where had it gotten me?" [1]

LaMotta broke down and agreed to take the Fox fight and lose it. For a man of great pride who believed in his own skills and never took a step back against anyone, this decision created great inner turmoil. The deal was a skewed one. LaMotta was promised the title shot, but then the mobsters turned the screws on him financially to obtain it. Although this came later, just to obtain that championship bout, LaMotta would have to pay $20,000 to handlers of middleweight champion Marcel Cerdan, guarantee Cerdan a return bout in case Jake won, and sign a personal services contract of three years duration with the International Boxing Club in New York (a.k.a., the mob). His payout for the title fight would be $19,000. That meant LaMotta's bribe payment was larger than his payday. This all illustrated how important getting his chance to win the crown was to LaMotta.

In addition, all of that was contingent on meeting and losing to Fox. There are not many incidents in LaMotta's life that make him a sympathetic figure, but this was one.

When someone is orchestrating a fix like the Fox match, it is paramount that the fight appear real, look good, be believable, and then be chalked up to being just another sporting upset. All the while, the wise guys bet on the underdog, which was sure to be Fox, and make a killing.

Early in training, LaMotta was sparring and his partner smacked him a good one in the belly. LaMotta was positive the punch broke a rib. When a doctor examined him, he told Jake the injury was to his spleen, that he could not fight, and his advice was to go home and rest. This was an out for Jake, a way to conveniently back out of the Fox bout and his deal with the mob. Joey LaMotta planned to notify Madison Square Garden officials about the injury ASAP, but Jake would not let him. He kept the injury quiet.

Mentally, LaMotta could not comfortably prepare for the fight. He was so distraught by his forced circumstances that he constantly second-guessed himself for agreeing to the fix. He argued in his head repeatedly about the situation, whether he should change his mind or go ahead with the deal. He had been forced into a hard place and had difficulty coping with it because, for now, he was his own enemy. LaMotta was haunted by the Fox fix before he even committed the crime.

Worse, the odds on the fight shifted because bookies heard whispers the fight was not on the up-and-up. Some stopped taking bets altogether.

"In case you don't know, something like that [talk of a fix] gets around the world I live in like lightning," LaMotta said. "They [bookies] got a sense of smell about things like that." [2]

Ironically, for someone who would later become an actor, LaMotta could not put on a good performance in the ring against Fox to make things look genuine. This was no doubt because LaMotta was so torn about what he was doing. He had only been known to fight one way in the ring, as the guy making the action. He took punishment against better fighters to give punishment. He had never been off his feet in a fight.

LaMotta occasionally lost fights, but he didn't know how to lose deliberately. He had always shown pride and determination in the ring, so he didn't know how to look bad on purpose. Although LaMotta went through with the bout, complete with his spleen problem, he looked so terrible in the ring fans suspected foul play. A guy who had been so genuine, it had worked to his detriment all his life, could not pull off being a phony for a half hour. The LaMotta–Fox match was bad theatre.

At a time when mobsters had a stranglehold on the sport of boxing, Jake LaMotta could not get a deserved shot at the middleweight championship without engaging in a fixed-fight loss to Billy Fox.

When the bell rang and LaMotta marched to the center of the ring to engage Fox, he learned he was so much better than the intended winner he didn't know what to do.

"I don't know how we even got through the first round without me murdering him," LaMotta said. "Sometimes I thought the air from my punches was affecting him. I began to panic a little. I was supposed to be throwing a fight to this guy and it looked like I was going to end up holding him on his feet." [3]

Enough of a show was made that Fox won by technical knockout at 1 minute 47 seconds of the fourth round. The stink and recriminations began almost immediately. LaMotta hadn't been that convincing a loser, although he tried to explain things away by noting anyone can have a bad day.

"I don't know how long it's been since you stood up on a platform and listened to about 20,000 people booing you, but I personally didn't like it," LaMotta said. "And the knowledge that I deserved it didn't help." [4]

LaMotta said he learned there is more than one way to fix a fight and he was too stupid to do it the right way. That is, not making everyone in the known world suspicious. He did such a lousy job that the New York State Athletic Commission and the local district attorney began investigating and the fight purse was held up.

When hearings were conducted, however, LaMotta's doctor testified that he had entered the ring with a ruptured spleen. For public consumption, it was said that Fox landed a good blow on the spleen early in the fight and that affected LaMotta throughout. The investigation of the fight being fixed went away. However, Jake was fined $1,000 and suspended from fighting for seven months for basically keeping the injury quiet.

Suspicions about what truly happened followed LaMotta throughout that half-year-plus suspension and for years afterwards, although for various stretches of time he made them go away. LaMotta considered the Fox incident the worst stain on his career; he was tormented by it and felt guilty for the rest of his life.

Not giving your all, not being honest with the public, and throwing a decision all added up to committing the cardinal sin of boxing. LaMotta squirmed free of the bind he was in, for a long time living behind the excuse of the injured spleen. He lost fans who no longer believed in him, but they may have questioned their own skepticism later when he got back into action and resumed fighting, all which led up to the long-awaited title shot.

LaMotta was bitter that he was forced into such an untenable situation where his entire career could have rotted away without ever getting a shot at the middleweight title if he had not sold his soul to the devil. In his mind, and in the minds of many others, that's where the true crime lay. How was it in the first place that such an unscrupulous group of criminals could control access to the world title?

In 1960, LaMotta was required to testify in front of a U.S. Senate subcommittee investigating mafia involvement in boxing about what transpired in the Fox fight and the dealings that surrounded it. LaMotta unloaded his guilty conscience by telling the truth about the entire sordid manner. This Washington, D.C., appearance was a cleansing of sorts for LaMotta. He had kept the secret for 13 years, playing along with the fiction that the loss to Fox was due to his spleen more than his psyche or a premeditated evil scheme. The revelations were powerful.

That lay years in the future, however. The critical years of LaMotta's boxing career now spread before him. The path was cleared for him to fight for a title at long last. Now, it was up to his fists to grab it.

10

Pugilist at Home

While his career followed this tentative path, Jake LaMotta was difficult to be around at home. He and Vikki had their differences. There was no doubt LaMotta was possessive and jealous. But beyond that, his wife grew to fear him. In LaMotta's own autobiography, he quotes Vikki telling his best friend Pete how she was being crushed by his omnivorous personality, fueled by his intense and insane jealousy.

"You were telling me once about how he doesn't trust anybody," the book *Raging Bull* quoted Vikki in conversation with Pete saying, "not even his own brother. Well, he doesn't trust me, either, and I'm his wife. It's like living in a goddamned jail, I tell you. I can't even breathe without him wanting to know why. If he even thinks I have a wrong thought, he uses me for a punching bag." [1]

That brought the ugly truth out in the open. The top contender for the middleweight title of the world, a man whose fists were his livelihood, beat his wife.

Vikki was 22 and told Pete she wanted a little bit of fun out of life, not spending it feeling as if she was a prisoner. She suggested she did not love Jake as much as she used to, but said, "He's just punched the love out of me. I'm afraid of him. I'm not joking when I say I'm afraid he'll lose his temper so bad someday that he really will kill me." [2]

That did not sound like a love match. If it had ever been, it seemed the good feelings had vanished, at least on Vikki's part. There was probably no easy way to explain Jake's thinking. To listen to Vikki, though, Jake was a leading candidate for wife abuser of the year.

LaMotta treasured Vikki and smothered her. He displayed her and imprisoned her. When they first were introduced, LaMotta could not believe a woman that good looking said she wanted to meet him. The inner Jake told him he was a pug. Yet, there are pictures of LaMotta in the ring from his youth and his prime where it is easy to see how a woman could find him sexy. He had thick, wavy hair, a muscular body, and brought menace into the ring. A young woman might look at LaMotta and see a man who exuded power and would always be able to protect her.

Vikki came along when LaMotta was in the limelight and getting bigger. She bore him children and did not seem to mind being a bauble on his arm when he visited nightclubs and made appearances in New York. Still, there was something missing in her life. She was still growing up when she met LaMotta, and as she moved into her twenties, she became, or wanted to become, more of her own woman. She did not want to be known only as the little woman at home.

There may have been a time when the sassy teenager accepted LaMotta's word for everything, but she outgrew that stage. Of all things, Vikki seemed to want the marriage to be a partnership. LaMotta was way too old-fashioned and insecure for that type of relationship. He was the man of the house, the one who wore the pants in the family, and he was in charge. Sure, he could go out and drink and live it up, but if for some reason Vikki did not answer the phone at home, he imagined all sorts of violation of trust.

When he outlined his life with the opposite sex in *Raging Bull*, LaMotta talked of being able to get just about any babe in the neighborhood. He had a name and an allure, plus his good buddy Pete Savage was good at attracting women who wanted to go out with the fighter.

After Vikki came into the picture and LaMotta became a married man with children, he was beholden to her. He should have been content at home. However, LaMotta was never content for very long. He was very much a restless soul, a worried man who carried his insecurities around with him everywhere he traveled, as if he had packed them in a suitcase along with a pair of pajamas.

He was always on edge, wondering if he would ever get a shot at the middleweight title. He always felt guilty about Harry the bookie. Believing he had murdered him, the entire stupid incident weighed on him, and he did not go to confession of any type to tell anyone. Pete always knew, from the night the attempted robbery happened, but he was not someone to pour your heart out to even if you were desperate. LaMotta felt he never could talk about such an intimate problem with his wife.

Surprisingly, it was easier for LaMotta to confess to occasional sexual impotence in his autobiography than to bring his wife into his confidence about the worst sin of his past. It was remarkable on many levels that he managed to talk of it in print, although surely, he never would have if he had not learned that Harry survived. There is no statute of limitations for murder, so LaMotta, ashamed as he was by what he did by smashing the man in the head, would never have included the incident in the book if there was a possibility he still might have been tried and taken to jail for it.

Vikki was the girl of LaMotta's dreams, but he didn't really comprehend that after their initial dating and early marriage days. LaMotta could have been capable of living happily ever after with Vikki if he had run his life a little bit better. He had four daughters and two sons, some by different wives, and he lost both sons tragically. Three of those kids were Vikki's children.

LaMotta enjoyed the idea of being a father, but the childrearing was pretty much Vikki's responsibility. LaMotta was the worst example of a man who took his work home with him. When things were tough, he was tense. When he was tense, he took it out on anybody nearby.

When he was a teenaged predator prowling the neighborhood looking for early marks to rob, LaMotta was a punk with no conscience. He usually led with his emotion, whether it was an appropriate one or not. It was his way of fighting back against the world when it was cruel to him or his family. Throughout his boxing years, LaMotta never outgrew that stage of development. He took personally everything that went wrong, unable to sort out personal slights from just-the-way-things-are. It was not easy being Jake LaMotta when the whole world was against you. He was paranoid, but deservedly so on some fronts, especially as it related to his career. There were people in power explicitly holding him back, preventing him from claiming his due of having a legitimate chance to fight for the middleweight crown.

What LaMotta was never able to do was to step back from the vice grip the mob had on his title aspirations to see the blessings in his life, his wife and children. LaMotta's was a life led like a jet plane always flying into turbulence. Vikki met Jake in at the neighborhood swimming pool. Whereas once her father was the strictest of jerks in determining her hours, by the time she began dating Jake, he seemed not to care about anything she did at whatever hour, even though she was yet to turn 16. Jake buttered up the father by giving him Havana cigars which were, according to Vikki, one of her father's few true pleasures in life.

In the beginning, as is the case in almost all love matches, things were beautiful.

"But the nicest thing about being with Jake was that being with me seemed to make him happy," Vikki said. "Whenever he saw me, his face seemed to light up. No matter where we were, his eyes were always on me." [3]

New love is supposed to be sweet like that. LaMotta was mesmerized by Vikki's stunning good looks and that this beautiful babe wanted to be with him. He never wanted to let her go. That's why he insisted they get married when Vikki got pregnant. Despite her misgivings about long-term life with Jake and marrying anyone at 16, she went through with it in 1946.

The newly married couple set up housekeeping in Jake's New York apartment. It was a tad on the cozy side because LaMotta was not rolling in dough. He fought often and made decent purses for the time, but the truly big money eluded him the way his chance at the title always did. Those two things, of course, were connected in the boxing world. The greater the fame and the ability to march into the ring carrying the championship belt over one's head, the more money the headliner was paid.

Vikki soon discovered that dating Jake was one thing, but living with him full-time was another. She had a misguided appreciation for what she took as sentimentality in his soul, believing that the youth who had skulked about the neighborhood committing crimes was not the same person as the man she married. On one level that was true, but perhaps she was naïve in thinking that a man whose profession involved beating people up was a gentleman underneath.

"When Jake and I got married, I didn't realize how deeply embedded his roots were in violence," Vikki said. "I knew about his past as a delinquent, but on the surface, at least, he seemed to regret it. I knew he was tough, but I was used to that. I came from a tough neighborhood." [4]

Vikki chose to read too much into a story about how when Jake, driving with his father, hit a boy who darted into the street in front of the car; they scooped him up, rushed him to the hospital, and tried to save him. After the boy died, LaMotta gave his entire earnings from his next fight to the boy's family as a gesture of sorrow and atonement. Despite all that, Vikki said Jake was always haunted by the boy's death. Using this as a prime example, Vikki said the Jake she first knew was "protective of little people." [5]

The new Mrs. LaMotta said the first year of the marriage was a good one after she got used to being married. She said Jake was a good cook, and they hosted dinner parties together. They dined with Jake's family, and she hit it off with Jake's father. She and Jake went to the movies, horseback riding, and for long walks in the snow. He patiently taught Vikki how to drive. This all sounds like an alien Jake to the rest of the world, but during this period, his young bride loved sharing these activities. On occasion, LaMotta would shower her with spontaneous gifts of $100, sometimes in $1 bills, just to go buy clothes. He was a man in love and called Vikki "pretty baby," she said. "I was his doll." [6]

Because Vikki was so young, she never gave a moment's thought to the way Jake dictated the relationship, took the role of adult making all the decisions, and dictated her opinions on other subjects, too. At first, a youthful Vikki did not mind any of that. Marriage was a pretty chauvinistic institution in the mid-1940s, so this was not especially out of the ordinary for how many couples lived. It may, however, have been a bit more extreme because Vikki had a woman's body and a teenager's maturity, and Jake wanted to keep things exactly the way they were.

Over time, as Vikki aged and grew up a little despite Jake's best efforts, she began to question how they were living. She said everyone knew LaMotta was jealous, but that word did not sufficiently describe his outlook. Jealous was only the easy description.

"But it was more than that," Vikki said. "He was all-consuming. He lived as part of me. If I went to visit my mother or father, Jake had to be there. If I wanted to speak to someone, Jake was at my side. If I needed groceries, Jake wanted to go to the store with me. If the telephone rang, Jake had to answer it. Every aspect of my life was under his control." [7]

Young Vikki didn't mind initially. She read his behavior only as more examples of how much LaMotta loved her. But then he did not want her to have any money, saying he would go with her and pay. Next, he did not even want her to talk to service men, such as butchers, because they were guys. Vikki nearly flipped when LaMotta did not want her to talk to female friends without him being within earshot, either.

It all became stifling and suffocating. This gradually drove a schism between the couple, and years later when Vikki and Jake sometimes crossed paths (in some minor way, she always periodically popped up in his life), Vikki said she asked him why he had behaved in such an iron-fisted and controlling manner. He responded by saying, "I didn't want you to be with other people because I thought they'd put ideas in your head. I wanted to train you, so you only knew what I wanted you to know." It sounded a bit like living under a Communist regime behind the Iron Curtain. [8]

"That was Jake," Vikki said. "I was a possession, the prize he was afraid to let anyone touch." [9]

Vikki became Mrs. LaMotta not long before Jake got the offer he couldn't refuse from the mob, the one that set him up with Billy Fox. The way she describes the months of Jake's frustration passing without the chance to win a championship it sounds as if overtures, perhaps tinged somewhat with threats, were constantly being delivered to Jake. His brother Joey was mostly the conduit. He would talk to the mobsters and present the offer to Jake, urging him to accept. Jake would refuse and continue fighting, running his own career his own way, even though he was guiding it down a dead-end street.

It took a great mental toll on LaMotta. He wanted to win the title on the level. He was not scared of any opponent and wanted to beat them all on the level. Years had passed, however, and he had been shut out. Some referred to him as "The People's Champion." Others called LaMotta, "The Uncrowned Champion." Bah, he didn't care about such sobriquets. He wanted to be known as the real champion, to have the prized belt wrapped around his waist. This made him both a man of principle, but also a hopeless case.

These were regular forays. Joey, who lived across the street being the messenger (Pete was in prison during some of this time), kept telling Jake he would get his title fight, but he had to take a dive.

"The thing he was proudest of," Vikki said of Jake, "was being an honest fighter." [10]

This was a laudable stand. Frequently, men buckle under to pressure and bribes even though they know they are doing wrong. LaMotta's conscience was otherwise not completely clean, so he had much to gain by being an honest man here. But, he came of age as a fighter when neither principle, nor fairness, ruled. So that meant he had much to lose, being at risk of becoming a footnote in middleweight boxing history rather than a bold-faced name in the record book designating him as a champ. No wonder LaMotta was tortured.

The gangsters hammered at LaMotta over and over, sending forward deals urging and pressuring him to throw the fight to Billy Fox. Consistent with his day-to-day approach of living with Vikki, Jake did not share all his thinking at the time. At last, he caved in and made the deal to fix the Fox fight in 1947. This occurred a year into his marriage to Vikki. LaMotta did not confer with her, nor tell her what he was talking to Joey about. Vikki heard enough on her own to know that some heat was on her husband.

She was aware Jake was going to fight Fox on November 14, 1947. She was also aware when LaMotta injured his spleen. She witnessed Joey telling Jake to use the spleen as an excuse for the loss. However, a couple of days before the scheduled bout, she thought there was as much chance Jake would pull out because of the spleen injury as he would go through with the fight.

She never thought Jake was capable of such serious action as throwing a fight. He was too proud. He had turned down the same kind of offer many times. Repeatedly LaMotta had made it clear by his actions and words that he wanted nothing to do with the mobsters who desired to run his life. Vikki was 17, and not wise to the inner workings of the corrupt echelons of the sport. She hadn't been around long and had no knowledge of how matches were made.

"Jake never told me he threw the fight," Vikki said. At that time, "knowing how proud he was to be a fighter, I never dreamed he'd do it. Maybe I was naïve. Maybe I shut my eyes to what was going on around me." [11]

Vikki said she did not learn for certain that Jake threw the fight to Billy Fox in 1947 until 13 years later. By 1960, Jake LaMotta was retired, and the LaMottas were divorced.

11

Marcel Cerdan

The beloved French champion boxer Marcel Cerdan was born July 22, 1916, in the portion of the country that later became independent and known as Algeria. Many of his countrymen believe Cerdan was the greatest fighter ever produced by France. His parents were French, but living in Sidi Bel-Abbès, part of the Algerian French colony at the time. The population there was mostly Arabic, with a minority of French colonizers.

When Cerdan, who was 5'7" began his professional career in 1934, he was mostly based in Morocco and French Algeria. He learned his skills in North Africa, inspired by his older brothers who boxed. Cerdan was just 17 years old when he made his debut.

The eventual middleweight champion won his first 47 fights. After his first loss, Cerdan won five more fights in a row and took a 52-1 record into a challenge for the European welterweight title against Saviello Turiello in Milan, Italy. Cerdan won the 147-pound continental crown. He then promptly reeled off another 23 straight victories. At the time, it was more difficult for a European fighter to gain a chance at winning a world title, so it made sense to stay very active and build eye-catching records.

During his ascent, Cerdan gained some intriguing nicknames. One was "The Moroccan Bomber." The other was "The Casablanca Clouter." Dark-haired and handsome, Cerdan fought regularly in Paris before the outbreak of World War II and before the Germans marched into the capital city and overwhelmed it, installing the Vichy government.

Unlike Jake LaMotta, with whom the final stages of his career would be intertwined, Cerdan did enlist in the service during World War II, but also kept fighting in the boxing ring during the war years. Cerdan was 23 years old in 1940 when he signed up for the French army, just as Germany was poised to invade.

The Germans swiftly overran the country and Cerdan offered his services to the Allies. Still, Cerdan managed to squeeze in bouts during the war. Considering the broader circumstances, Cerdan fought often. After 1942, Cerdan did not continue his boxing career in Paris, but was essentially based in Algiers. He made one foray to Casablanca and then fought several times in Italy.

Some have said Cerdan did not fight for four years during the war, but the record books say differently. He is credited with eight bouts in 1942, six in 1943, and eight in 1944. He won all but one of them, losing to Victor Buttin by disqualification in Algiers on August 15, 1942.

Allied troops liberated Paris on August 25, 1944. From then onward, the Germans were ousted and the country began its attempts at renewal. Cerdan's first boxing match back in Paris took place on March 9, 1945. By the end of that year, Cerdan was campaigning as a middleweight, for him the higher weight class of 160. On November 30, he captured the French middleweight title by knocking out Assane Diouf in Paris in three rounds. An extremely experienced fighter, Diouf was eight years older than Cerdan, with a career record of 77-36-11.

Although they were on opposite sides of the Atlantic Ocean with World War II still raging (the Battle of the Bulge and D-Day were still to come), and although the Germans were retreating towards Berlin, Marcel Cerdan and Jake LaMotta were fighting their own private wars in their home countries.

Although each harbored the ambition of becoming middleweight champion of the world, neither LaMotta nor Cerdan probably knew very much about the other. If so, it was because their names may have appeared in *The Ring* magazine and they accidentally caught notice of it. Soon enough, however, they would begin to play absolutely huge roles in one another's lives.

Meanwhile, in a country wracked by war, a boxer was no hero in 1945. Being a soldier, or even more impressively, being a general like Charles de Gaulle who helped to guide his pining countrymen in absentia as head of the French Republic while Germans ran roughshod over the land, was far more important to the nation.

De Gaulle was the leader of Free France between 1940 and 1944, and then in charge of the provisional government in 1944 and 1945 before being elected president of the new republic after war's end. Nation-building was required in tenuous times. It was worthwhile to cultivate French achievers in a country that boasted strong national identity and characteristics.

France was regarded by much of the world as a carefree nation indulgent in wine, women, and song. Boxers did not rate quite so high in the pantheon. There was no grand tradition of great fighters of French heritage, but the French did admire celebrities, A-listers, and eventually Cerdan stormed the public consciousness in that way.

If there is one other French boxer going down through history who rivaled Cerdan in accomplishment and in being well-appreciated, it was Georges Carpentier. Carpentier was born in 1894 and was a pilot during World War I. He was awarded two major French medals for his gallantry, which certainly added to his appeal.

Known as "The Orchid Man," Carpentier turned professional in 1908 and fought until 1924. He campaigned at several weight classes, beginning at welterweight (147 pounds), and made stops in all classes up through heavyweight, including light-heavyweight (175 pounds) during his 109 bouts.

Carpentier measured a shade less than 6' tall. As his body filled out with age, he was able to adapt to the larger weight divisions. His lifetime record was 88-14-6 with one no contest. On June 24, 1912, Carpentier challenged American Frank Klaus for the world middleweight title, and he lost by disqualification. Eight years later in Jersey City, New Jersey, Carpentier won the light-heavyweight crown by knocking out champ Battling Levinsky seven seconds into the fourth round.

It was a career highlight for a future vaudeville song and dance man and short-term film actor who had gone through a world war before he could capture a world title. In September 1922, Carpentier lost the crown to Battling Siki in Paris, unable to utilize a home-ring advantage.

However, Carpentier made bigger news in between. In a move that one does not see in this modern era of fighting, rather than defending the light-heavyweight title soon after he won it, Carpentier pitted himself against legendary heavyweight champ Jack Dempsey in his next bout. This was a fight that grabbed worldwide attention and enhanced Carpentier's reputation if not his career. In July 1921, Dempsey knocked out Carpentier in four rounds in Jersey City.

Because both men were world champions, promoter Tex Rickard hyped the gate by declaring the Dempsey–Carpentier bout "The Fight of the Century." It was early in the century and a similar phrase since has been applied to many bouts of the twentieth century. Whatever Rickard said, there was magic in the promotion. Dempsey–Carpentier became boxing's first million-dollar fight, producing a gate that approached $1.8 million. As a trivia fact, this was the first major fight women were allowed to attend. Until then, big-time boxing in the United States was a stag affair.

Dempsey, a.k.a., "The Manassa Mauler," was not terribly popular in his home country at the time. Unlike Carpentier, who gained bonus points for his service, Dempsey did not fight during World War I and in some quarters, was considered a draft dodger. Despite being a foreigner, Carpentier was viewed as a good guy and popular rooting choice.

Image-wise, the heavyweight champ may have looked like a bully compared to Carpentier as well. Dempsey weighed in at 188 pounds, while Carpentier didn't even approach the light-heavyweight limit, weighing in at 168 pounds. However, fans were provoked to a frenzy in the second round when Carpentier leveled Dempsey with a right to the jaw. Dempsey beat the count to his feet, and two rounds later finished off Carpentier. The Frenchman went down valiantly.

In 1924, trying to prove himself worthy of another shot at the heavyweight title, Carpentier was stopped in the 15th round on a technical knockout handed to him by Gene Tunney, Dempsey's nemesis. *The Ring* magazine voted that bout its best fight of the year. At age 30, Carpentier was closing in on the end of his career. Despite his excellent showing versus Tunney, he fought just four more times. One was a draw and another was a loss to Tommy Loughran. Loughran, who won 121 fights, was regarded as one of the best light-heavyweight champs of all time.

That was enough for Carpentier and he was an anomaly in French boxing until Cerdan came along. It took time, but Cerdan's popularity eventually rivaled, and perhaps exceeded, Carpentier's. Through his achievements, good looks, and personality, Cerdan managed to transcend his sport to become a public figure in France.

Of course, Cerdan needed to add something critical to his résumé that Carpentier had—a world championship. It took years of fighting for him to gain an opportunity, but on September 21, 1948, Cerdan was finally granted a shot. The middleweight champion was the indomitable Tony Zale, who had an all-comers mentality and oftentimes took on the same comer numerous times.

Zale had knocked out Rocky Graziano, LaMotta's old pal from Coxsackie, to lift the crown. When Zale and Cerdan met, the site was the old Roosevelt Stadium in Jersey City. By then, Cerdan had compiled a 109-3 record, which is a lot of fights and a lot of wins without receiving a chance to win a world title. Cerdan couldn't have been readier. The bout was a slugfest. Both men were known for having the heart of a lion. This time it was Cerdan who imposed his will. Zale was an 8-5 favorite in the fight. Cerdan stopped Zale officially in the 12th round when Zale did not answer the bell for that round, to at last win world title recognition.

Zale, who was 35 years old at the time, had just completed his 87th professional fight. He never boxed again. Cerdan, who had waited so long, was already 32, and no young champion. However, he quickly was feted as one. Champagne flowed in Paris—and probably in New Jersey, too.

One of the spectators was singer Edith Piaf, Cerdan's mistress and an international singing sensation. It was said she twisted a rosary in her hands as her man fought for his dream and that she prayed throughout the rounds.

Cerdan was a celebrity already, but now he became a bigger one, known to Frenchmen who didn't even follow boxing. He was on top of the world, fulfilled at last. He was married and had children, but Cerdan also had a visible love affair going with the famed Piaf, whose renown (at least until the moment of Zale's demise) eclipsed even his own.

Piaf, who was born in 1915, was an esteemed crooner who played nightclubs and cabarets, but progressed to an iconic national symbol. Her beginnings were sad and she lived in poverty as first her birth father abandoned her. Then her mother, who was a cabaret singer, also ditched her. Piaf was left with a grandmother who was a brothel Madame and raised her. It was hardly the most wholesome of environments, but Piaf learned to sing in the whorehouse and played the piano for the prostitutes and their clients. Eventually, Piaf sang on Paris streets, hoping to be paid in coins by passersby. Piaf grew no taller than 4'8", but she packed a wallop with her voice and was nicknamed "The Little Sparrow."

It was learned much later that the pint-sized singer with such a sweet voice was even sought out by the Nazis to entertain at their parties, but had secretly worked undercover for the French resistance during the war. Quietly, and through her contacts, Piaf had somehow helped arrange the escape of hundreds of Frenchmen from the Gestapo. She hid her spy role so well that initially Piaf was accused of being a collaborator. Even more than a half century after her 1963 death, Piaf is revered by her countrymen. That fame and her music have endured in France, but it has also spread widely. Her name is known to many music aficionados worldwide and born long after her death.

Although she came to stardom during the German occupation of France, Piaf was still able to flourish. By 1944, Piaf was playing the Moulin Rouge and was romantically linked to singer and actor Yves Montand.

In 1945, Piaf wrote and performed her most exalted tune, "La Vie En Rose," (Life Is Pink), which was ultimately bestowed a Grammy Hall of Fame award in 1998. Although Piaf essentially drank herself to death at 47 in 1963, some 100,000 people attended her funeral. She remains venerated.

Despite any previous affairs, there is little doubt the love of Piaf's life was Cerdan, their love affair beginning in 1948. Despite his marriage and role as father to three children, theirs was no clandestine affair. All of France was aware of their relationship.

As someone whose first language was French, Cerdan was not often quoted in English, but one thing memorably attributed to him was actually from a movie about him. His piece of advice in the movie? "Don't be satisfied with half-measures." [1] Since the film was made in 2007, it is not clear if he truly made the statement.

Cerdan's affair with Piaf heated up as he was working his way to his long-awaited chance to wrest the middleweight title from whoever held it at the moment. It so happened that the opponent was Zale. Perhaps if the current title-holder was someone else, Cerdan would have been bypassed. Zale never ducked anyone in his life, and when they shared the ring for nearly 12 rounds, Zale could not duck Cerdan's punches.

Although some time had passed since LaMotta made his deal with mobsters and threw the fight to Billy Fox in exchange for a chance to fight for the middleweight title, the shot finally did come around. After the roulette wheel stopped spinning, the ball landed on Marcel Cerdan's name as LaMotta's opponent.

Having the champ of the moment be Cerdan for LaMotta rather than Zale was likely good for the sport since Zale was getting a little shopworn. Still, Cerdan–Zale beforehand provided a flavorful allure. Cerdan had fought often enough in the United States to be a known quantity. Zale, the man he beat, was widely respected.

Even if some suggested Zale might have been over the hill, the doubters could not argue with the fact that in Zale's previous bout he had KO'd Rocky Graziano. Cerdan's lengthy experience and barrel full of wins gave him credibility, too.

As far as LaMotta was concerned, he had been wandering in the desert for what seemed like 40 years so he didn't care who the other guy was in the ring as long as the championship belt was up for grabs. He wasn't fighting Edith Piaf, he was fighting a middleweight champ with more than 100 wins. LaMotta wasn't going to exchange bon mots in French with Cerdan, he was going to exchange punches with him.

"This was extra special on account of the fact that Cerdan was a Frenchman," LaMotta said. "Americans are so used to taking it for granted that they're the only top-ranked fighters, at least from the class of, say welterweight on, that when a real top-notch foreign fighter comes along, there's a special atmosphere built up. A fight like that builds and builds till finally it's the night of the fight, the hour of the fight, and almost the minute of the fight, and now here's the time you've been waiting for ever since—well, in my case, ever since I can remember, ever since I was a kid." [2]

LaMotta was not the only one who believed his shot at the title was overdue. He did not like many of the sportswriters who covered his bouts and did not count any of them as friends, but he did like some of the things written about him, especially when the words agreed with his own thoughts.

At this particular time as LaMotta piled up win after win in the 1940s, he accepted analysis of his career as the number one contender, or as the uncrowned champion, as his due. He just hated the comments because they did not read, "Middleweight champion of the world."

In November 1946 before the Billy Fox fight and long before the title fight against Cerdan, *The Ring* magazine wrote a story about LaMotta that was as complimentary as could be without penning it himself. The first paragraph read, "Acclaimed by *The Ring*, a newspaper poll, and the National Boxing Association as the number one challenger for the middleweight championship, Jake LaMotta is waiting on the New York State Athletic Commission to recognize his claim." [3] Also predicted in the story, "The time is not far distant, however, when the Bronx assassin will be there winging for the coveted crown." [4]

Clearly the author was misinformed or misled, or simply felt fair play was inevitable, which was not true. The time was indeed still far distant. LaMotta–Cerdan did not take place until two-and-a-half years after that article hit the newsstands.

LaMotta, as he well knew and understood, even while reading the optimistic words in 1946, that he might be waiting until doomsday for that title bout if he didn't cave in and do business with the mob.

On and on the article went, extolling LaMotta's virtues with thick praise. "He has the killer instinct of Jack Dempsey and that's saying a mouthful. In all his 71 professional starts, Jake has yet to disappoint the fans. No one has ever knocked him down and he has proven his worth under fire. He is tireless and has plenty of heart." [5]

The Ring was the bible of boxing, but who was reading it? No one could blame LaMotta if he turned his eyes heavenward and asked God, "Why not me?"

The man with little patience had to be patient for many more months after those compliments were lathered upon his reputation because those in charge in the boxing world were not god-fearing men who did not believe in fair play.

12

Prepping for the Title

Jake LaMotta held up his end of the bargain with the gangsters by throwing his fight with Billy Fox. But he did such a terrible job of acting like a legitimate boxer in the ring that his performance created suspicion across the sport.

Now that LaMotta was supposedly free of his obligation to the mob, he should have been in line for a middleweight title shot. However, LaMotta's inability to fake his showing more convincingly gummed up the works, at least temporarily.

In his own mind, he could have taken Fox out at will, and it was against not only his principles, but his entire core not to punch out his opponent. Oh, it bothered Jake. Yet, once he did the deed, he was not completely free and clear to pursue a title shot.

For one thing, it wouldn't look good after all these years of beating other guys to suddenly fight for the crown after a loss.

Much worse, the stench of LaMotta's in-ring actions put all types of officials on his trail to see if something was amiss in the fight. The same authorities who had never stepped in to help LaMotta when he was wrongly being shut out of a title opportunity now jumped in to investigate him and find out if he had cut a nefarious deal.

First came the district attorney's office of New York. Next came the New York State Athletic Commission. They were all sniffing around LaMotta, trying to determine if the bout that seemed to stink all the way to Staten Island was, in reality, garbage.

LaMotta wasn't much of an actor in the ring when he was supposed to be reeling from the punishment dished out by Fox. He didn't know how to react to punches that didn't hurt him. He had spent his entire adult life trying to stay out of trouble in the boxing ring, and then he had to act as if he was hurting, in pain, about to go down, when nothing of the sort was true.

The key to LaMotta's limited exoneration was the spleen injury he suffered working out in the lead-up to the fight. He really shouldn't have been in the ring, and when a doctor testified that it was likely the spleen issue is what made Jake look so bad during the fight, the officials bought it. He was a licensed source and they weren't about to call the doctor a liar.

However, going ahead with the fight when injured, even if some would call that bravery, was actually a violation of the rules. In a manner of speaking, it was a fraud on the public. An injured fighter being less than 100 percent healthy might not be able to give a solid accounting. Because LaMotta hid the injury, he was penalized. Jake's punishment was a $1,000 fine and a seven-month suspension. However, by taking the rap for concealing the spleen problem, LaMotta avoided a potentially much more severe punishment for throwing the fight.

Vikki, Jake's wife, was still essentially in his thrall. It wasn't until many years later that she realized Jake had fixed the Fox bout. When she wrote a book about her life, she dredged up some of the newspaper commentary that followed the bout. There was a passel of newspapers in New York City at the time, and they all had someone covering the fights. These writers all seemed to weigh in with their thoughts, dropping hints that stopped short of libel, but nonetheless making the point they felt something was strange in the ring.

Vikki LaMotta strung together several passages, quoting the writers about what they saw in LaMotta versus Fox. "The battle was attended by many strange developments, not the least of which was a flood of reports in advance that it would not be waged on its merits. LaMotta's fighting style, or lack of it, was another strange incident," said the *New York Times*. "LaMotta never fought as foolishly as he did last night. Every move he made might have been ordered by Fox. [LaMotta's showing was] feeble and mysterious," reported the *New York Daily Mirror*. "LaMotta seemingly asked for it as early as the second round when he stuck his chin out and invited Fox to hit it," argued the *New York Post*. "He was a poor actor, slamming away with mock ferocity in the first round at Fox's body. This naturally invited shots by Fox at LaMotta's open jaw. LaMotta is not that much of a raw amateur," the *New York Daily News* chimed in.[1]

Surely fight fans who were not present at ringside got the message. "Hold your nose over this one, folks."

"Jake had lost fights before," Vikki said. "I'm sure he thought Billy Fox would be just another loss, that he could throw the fight quietly, pick up an IOU from the mob and go on to challenge for the world middleweight championship. But it had been too obvious."[2]

It should be remembered that Vikki made those observations with 20-20 hindsight, decades in the future. But, she also seemed right on.

LaMotta was in no mood to be idle for seven months for his suspension. But, he had to put up with the situation, and be glad the doctor was a stand-up guy who told the truth and that nobody else officially ratted him out about the fix. These were bad times for Jake. He became known in his neighborhood (and in some others) as "Jake the Fake." That wounded him.

In Vikki's memory, her husband was a wreck during his enforced layoff, not knowing what to do with himself and distraught over his predicament.

"The next seven months were among the worst of Jake's life," she said. "He stayed indoors, alone, and wouldn't talk to anybody. He refused to go out because he was ashamed to be seen on the streets. He was a changed person, horribly depressed and unhappy with life." [3]

From November 1947 to June 1948, LaMotta did not box for pay. He resumed his career with a bout on June 1, 1948, against Ken Stribling. LaMotta fought nine times before the middleweight title match with Marcel Cerdan was set for June 1949. There was quite a bit of distance on the calendar between Fox and Cerdan.

Not all of those bouts were gimmes and not all of them were victories, either. LaMotta beat Stribling (33-14-3), Burl Charity (40-24-7), Johnny Colan (60-19-1), Vern Lester (25-27-16), Tommy Yarosz (81-10-1), Laurent Dauthuille (45-13-4), Robert Villemain (52-7-4), O'Neil Bell (21-13-5), and Joey DeJohn (74-14-2). It took split decisions to conquer Lester and Villemain, and LaMotta lost a unanimous decision to Dauthuille in Montreal.

The fight with Dauthuille, whose nickname was "The Tarzan of Buzenval" although he was born in France, took place in the Montreal Forum, home of the National Hockey League Canadiens. Dauthuille was very dangerous and could fight with anyone in the division at the time.

On February 21, 1949, Dauthuille was good enough to beat Jake LaMotta. Dauthuille's punching opened a very deep cut over Jake's eye that took 12 stitches to close, which could have derailed the express train to the title shot for LaMotta. Actually, since the Fox fight and the suspension, he had more or less been traveling by local train.

He was rightly worried the loss would once again shove him to the back of the line, but his brother Joey said he had spoken to "The Man" and been reassured that type of defeat would not cost him his opportunity. He was fortunate that time.

To LaMotta, the waiting was interminable. He had sold his soul, and he still had not seen any payback after two years. He watched the middleweight title change hands throughout the 1940s, the belt transferring between men whom LaMotta was certain he could defeat.

Tommy Yarosz was a past champ. He had possession of the middleweight crown in 1934 and 1935 and was on the downside of his career when LaMotta bested him late 1948. Then, following as champs were Eddie Babe Risko, Freddie Steele, Fred Apostoli, Solly Krieger, and Al Hostak before the 1930s ended. While LaMotta was clamoring for a shot, Ceferino Garcia, Ken Overlin, Billy Soose, and Tony Zale took turns wearing the belt. Rocky Graziano borrowed the crown, but Zale won it back before losing his furious bout with Cerdan.

All those men, over all of those years, seemed to be lined up to solely to deprive LaMotta of his birthright. Well, now it was time to rectify the mistakes of the past and nullify the previous boycott of him.

For all the angst the fix with Fox caused LaMotta, he was not truly free and clear to negotiate his own deal in the title shot. He had dissed the mobsters many times over the years, raising their ire. He had taken a long time in coming around to help them out. Always they had control of the big prize LaMotta wanted, and they dangled it in front of him. Numerous times he spurned the bad guys, virtually spitting in their eyes.

Oh, LaMotta would get his title shot, but there would be more strings attached. It would not just be a meeting between the champion and the number one–rated challenger. Brother Joey was sent to deliver the message to Jake that the time had come at last for him to take his swing at the title. LaMotta never thought he would hear those words—a chance. Just one chance is all he had ever asked for. It was due to him for all the blood, sweat, and tears he had invested in the sport. Yes, his turn had come.

LaMotta had put up with his forced layoff. He had battled his way through another whole line of guys. As he waited, LaMotta thought the fix had killed his chances once and for all, that now he would never get to fight for the crown. As the end of the suspension period approached, Joey came over the house one day. They were out front when he told LaMotta that he had received word from the gangsters that once Jake was back in action and had polished off a few guys, he would get his opportunity.

"This was it! This was my chance!" LaMotta said. "I jumped on Joey and began wrestling with him and we both went down on the grass." [4]

It was then that Joey told him there was a catch. Of course, there was a catch. When a champion puts the title on the line, he gets the lion's share of the purse. The challenger gets a good payday, often the biggest of his life, with the idea that his true cash reward comes later if he wins the championship.

Joey told Jake the catch was $20,000. Not that he would make $20,000 for the fight, which was not a huge purse to begin with, but that he would have to fork over $20,000 to the wise guys as part of the deal. It was pretty crazy, but there it was. He had to come through with the cash or his chance would go away.

So LaMotta went to the bank and paid up. He gave the $20,000 to Joey to deliver, and that was the last LaMotta heard about the payoff. He asked a few people if they got any money, and they said they did not. He always assumed the cash went to Marcel Cerdan's people to make certain the champ would fight him, but he never knew for sure.

At the time, said LaMotta, the challenger's share was a standard 20 percent. His share versus Cerdan was 15 percent. By then, LaMotta was willing to accept any indignity to get into the damned ring with the champion. On the side, though, accepting odds of 8-5 against him by bookies, LaMotta did place a $10,000 bet on himself to win. No one ever said he lacked confidence.

Although LaMotta continued to beat all the men put in front of him, his showing against Fox colored some of the newspaper reporting on those bouts. There were suggestions maybe they were not all legitimate. The same scribes with doubts about the Fox fight hinted these victories were not all to Jake's credit. He had brought this new wave of cynicism upon himself because of the way he mishandled the Fox bout.

Right around the time the Cerdan fight was scheduled, Jake and Vikki had a baby girl. It seemed things might be turning his way.

During the years of impatient waiting, LaMotta did develop a following. He was popular with fight fans in New York and Detroit especially. *The Ring* magazine always seemed to be in his corner. He earned the magazine's praise by always putting on a good show.

"LaMotta carries dynamite in both hands," one *Ring* commentary noted. "He weaves like Dempsey, rushes out of a crouch and hammers the body. Once he gets in there it takes a derrick to pry him loose from his opponent. LaMotta is built like a brick tenement house. He wades in from the first bell and keeps going at top speed every second he is in there." [5]

At long last, as the fight with Cerdan loomed closer and closer, LaMotta would be able to show his stuff with the entire world watching. This was the moment he was born for, the moment he had waited for, the moment so long in coming.

13

Fighting for the Championship

The site was Briggs Stadium in Detroit, home of baseball's Tigers. By 1949, LaMotta had put on nearly as many fan-pleasing, winning performances in Detroit as Hank Greenberg or Hal Newhouser.

June 16, 1949, was one of the best days of Jake LaMotta's life. He may have fallen in love often enough to marry seven times and he may have fathered several children, but if forced to pick his greatest day it seems certain LaMotta would choose this moment as his top contender.

LaMotta was less than a month shy of turning 28 years old, and it seemed as if he had coveted the middleweight boxing champion of the world for half that time. His career had followed so many twists and turns, his life had taken so many twists and turns, it seemed entirely possible this day would never come for him.

But on that day, Jake LaMotta climbed into the ring to face Marcel Cerdan, the Frenchman who was also a champion of bonhomie. Nobody was going to say that about LaMotta. He was not a hale fellow well met. He brooded, snarled, and swore at people. He regularly alienated those who had his best intentions at heart.

He was a fighter, a fighter who knew his job, and if he had not been forced to swallow his pride and yes, become Jake the Fake for one bout, he would best be known as being a guy who never took a step backward.

You could tell this was a special occasion for the LaMottas as Vikki was coming to the fight. Jake fought numerous times during the early years of their union. Vikki traveled to fights on the road, but when Jake went to the arena, she stayed at the hotel. She did not watch him throw leather in person, nor take punches to his face. Not that she had any illusions about what went on in a boxing ring or how brutal the sport could be. She just didn't need to watch up close and personal as another man hit her husband.

Yet, this time it was different. Jake wanted her there on the premises to witness his moment of triumph, something he was sure would happen.

"The morning of the Cerdan fight, Jake sat me down in our hotel suite and said, 'I want you at ringside,'" Vikki said. "'You have to be there. I've waited my entire life for this.' He was very calm, not at all nervous. He was waiting for Cerdan with the same anticipation that a child has waiting for Christmas. 'There's no chance I'll be hurt. I'm going to win.'"[1]

There were some prefight handler shenanigans leading up to the fight. Cerdan's group tried to play head games with LaMotta. They were so sure that the fighter, who often had to lose a considerable number of pounds to make weight, would not be able to do so on the day of the fight that they demanded the day-before-fight weigh-ins be eliminated. The feeling was that LaMotta was really a light-heavyweight and would have to starve himself down to the appropriate weight and not have time to beef up on the day of the match. That tactic failed. Initially opposed, LaMotta agreed to weigh in twice, and both times he was within the limit without difficulty. If the point was to psyche out LaMotta, it more likely irritated him, providing a little extra oomph to motivate him against Cerdan. LaMotta felt he had turned the tables when it came to psychological maneuvering.

"They figured on throwing a scare into me by their actions at the commission offices and their cry of unfairness,"

LaMotta said. "But now I've tossed the scare into them. I know it." [2]

Also on fight day before LaMotta left the hotel, Jake received a long-lost visitor in Father Joseph, who just had to be on the scene to see his old charge from Coxsackie where LaMotta learned to fight. LaMotta often tweaked the Catholic priest by calling him "Dad" instead of "Father," despite being told repeatedly not to do so. Of course, he said it again. "Dad! You made it! Great, great, great. Boy, am I glad to see you." [3]

LaMotta had obtained a ticket for Father Joseph and sent him a train ticket from New York to Detroit. Father Joseph thanked him for that, but he told Jake he would not have missed the event no matter how he found a ticket. It must have been a nostalgic moment for Father Joseph, thinking this was an example of one of the boys from prison making good with him playing a role in his life rehabilitation.

At the weigh-in the day before the bout, the announcement of LaMotta's weight was 159½ pounds. For Cerdan, it was 158. They were both lean and appropriately under the 160-pound limit. The fight attracted the multitudes. LaMotta had been a prince in waiting for a long time and done much to enhance his reputation in Detroit. Cerdan was the new king, riding high in the public eye in France. He wanted to perpetuate his success. Some 22,183 spectators attended.

What they saw was vintage ferocious Jake. He was again a lion, this time not only in terms of courage, but in terms of ravaging his foe. The bout was scheduled for 15 rounds, the championship distance. But this fight did not last into true championship territory—into the 11th round or longer. In some ways, it was decided in the opening three minutes when Cerdan suffered an injury to his left shoulder in a fall. This is often mentioned as a reason for Cerdan's defeat

When Jake LaMotta finally obtained
a chance to battle for the middleweight crown
he defeated French hero Marcel Cerdan.

Associated Press

and LaMotta's dominance, but LaMotta, too, incurred an injury in either the second round or the fifth round. (There were conflicting accounts from ringside.) In *The Ring* magazine's coverage of the fight, the sub-head under the main headline included this phrase: "New champion's left hand badly swollen." [4] The evaluation was that LaMotta broke the second knuckle on his hand.

Although LaMotta was a bruiser, very strong and tough, he had small hands, which are not an advantage in the fight game. They were also somewhat brittle. He never fought as if he favored them, throwing punches with abandon, but he did have a problem this time.

Bigger problems were faced, however, by Cerdan from the beginning. He spent the remainder of the evening seeking to cope with the damaged shoulder, later diagnosed as torn muscles. That led to an inability to throw jabs and bigger punches from the left side from the second round onward.

This was Cerdan's first defense of the title he had lifted from Zale, and in Europe, especially France, his reign was expected to be long. Instead, he was in trouble starting in the first round. Cerdan was an 8-5 favorite, but things went awry for the visitor shortly into the opening three-minute stanza. Later, Cerdan said he hurt his shoulder after he threw his first punch.

The two had been mixing it up, and before the end of the round, Cerdan was on the deck, thrown down by LaMotta after a flurry. Cerdan was desperately trying to clinch and neutralize a LaMotta onslaught, but LaMotta wanted to press the advantage. He was trying to shrug Cerdan off at first, but then the brief wrestling match enraged him. LaMotta mustered his strength to push Cerdan away, which is when Cerdan fell. Although some believed at first LaMotta had knocked down the Frenchman, rightly no knockdown was recorded. Referee Johnny Weber never began a 10-count. Instead he actually helped Cerdan back to his feet.

The infighting, with LaMotta in command, continued in the same vein. LaMotta never stopped swinging or boring in to pressure the champ, often landing on the body and with combinations to the head. Cerdan did use both hands for a while after the first, but as the fight wore on, he refrained from throwing lefts. However, in the second and third rounds, Cerdan was at his best, at least once rocking LaMotta with right-hand shots. At most, they only paused LaMotta's attack.

"From start to finish, this was a rousing battle," said famed commentator Don Dunphy in a later voiceover of the fight film.[5]

The New York Times referred to LaMotta as "the rock-ribbed, steel-jawed little warrior from New York's Bronx." [6]

With all the attention on Cerdan's fall and his resulting injury, some overlooked the fact that LaMotta nearly KO'd the champ right away with a left hook to the face that propelled him against the ropes. There were no fouls, and officials indicated it was a clean fight, if a tough one where punishment was meted out, with Cerdan on the receiving end.

Cerdan was bleeding from a sliced open area above his right eye before the end of the first round and bled from the bridge of his nose by the end of the second. In the third, though, Cerdan drew LaMotta's blood in the spot where he had suffered the cut inflicted by Laurent Dauthuille. This development seemed only to energize LaMotta, perhaps fearful if he leaked too much blood the bout would be stopped.

No one realized, however, that from then on it would be a war of attrition for Cerdan. Unable to mount a sustained attack, he remained wide open for LaMotta body shots and sharp punches to the head. Cerdan was out of offense and was into preservation mode by the fourth round. Whether it was the impossibility of planning an effective strategy because of his left shoulder problem, a stamina issue, or too much Jake, the longer the fight went the less sure of his capability Cerdan seemed to be.

The New York Times report indicated Cerdan seemed poised to topple over like an imploding building by the seventh round. "Cerdan was so weakened, he didn't know where his corner was as the seventh and eighth rounds ended," the story indicated. "Indeed, the eighth round found Cerdan in disorderly retreat that indicated clearly he would not last." [7] Such opinions and gut feelings have been proven wrong before as fighters rallied in the late rounds, but not this time. The prediction was right on.

"[LaMotta] stays close trying to muzzle Cerdan's right," Don Dunphy said on the tape.[8]

Cerdan was wobbly in the ninth round and in a frenzy of activity in his corner, Cerdan's handlers sought to pep up the champ and make him presentable for a late run. Instead, when the one-minute respite ended, Cerdan remained where he was, sitting on his stool, cared for by his men. Cerdan's seconds had appealed to the doctor to declare a no-contest based on Cerdan's shoulder problem. Manager Jo Longman refused to allow the Frenchman back out for the 10th round, but they took the loss before Cerdan adjourned to a hospital for a check-up.

Sports writing analysts balanced Cerdan's shoulder injury and LaMotta's hand injury and decided neither gained a serious advantage over the other because of those misfortunes.

"The end comes dramatically... when Cerdan can't answer the bell," said Don Dunphy.[9]

That led Weber to wave the fight over and to raise LaMotta's hand in victory. Officially, the bout entered the record books as a 10th-round technical knockout. Just about the sweetest words Jake LaMotta ever heard were uttered over the loudspeaker at that point as the announcer introduced him to the Detroit crowd as "The winner by a knockout and the new champion." [10]

LaMotta piled up the points on the scorecards of the referee, the judges, and impartial sports writing observers. He was way ahead heading into the 10th round. There was also some thinking that if Jake was hurt, he pretty much masked the pain and kept firing his jab and a stream of punches.

"Each personified gameness by his showing," *The Ring* noted. Yet LaMotta's ability to adjust based on what he saw after the fight began gained him admirers like *The Ring.* "From the very start of the bout, LaMotta became the aggressor and seldom did he give way to the defending champion. He switched from a body attack to a head attack, and when he saw that Cerdan's defense for the face was nil due to his inability to use his left, he played a tattoo such as he never before had attempted." [11]

Not only was this the victory LaMotta had long envisioned—although he did not care who the opponent would be—it was sweetened because Cerdan had compiled a phenomenal record, was favored and touted as a top fighter, and he had been chosen *The Ring*'s Fighter of the Year for 1948.

Associated Press

A beaming Jake LaMotta with his two prized possessions:
his championship belt and wife Vikki
(whom he did indeed consider a possession).

In a nice sense of theatre for a big bout, the long-time heavyweight champ, Joe Louis, who made his home in Detroit, presented the championship belt to LaMotta.

For once, Jake LaMotta was satisfied. He was now the middleweight champion of the world. That is one of the titles a man can gain that he carries with him for life—and into the afterlife. Once you have won a world title, you are a world champ. Not only that, but his lovely bride Vikki was there to see it all, to share the glory.

"And it was a thing of beauty to watch," Vikki said. "Jake had been born to win the middleweight championship of the world and that night he was overpowering. His attitude, his conditioning everything about him was perfect that night. His entire life had been aimed toward that moment." [12]

Vikki wrote candidly of the reward she planned for LaMotta later in the night after he won his crown and they drank champagne together. She said she had chosen a sexy outfit consisting of while silk stockings, a white string bikini, and Jake's new championship belt.

"In the morning I was branded with belt marks all over my body," she said.[13]

She made sure it was a night to remember for hubby.

That was part of the celebration LaMotta left out of *Raging Bull*, but he also had difficulty putting into proper words how he felt when he finally became the champ after such a long quest.

"I cannot describe exactly what I felt," LaMotta said. "I felt like, you know, God had given me the world. It was absolute pandemonium. There was booing, I could hear that, but the whole place was filled with cheering, cheering for me, the reform-school kid from the Bronx." [14]

LaMotta was joined by Vikki and Father Joseph in the ring, where he let his pent-up emotion free and began to cry. Imagine that, Jake LaMotta shedding tears of joy. Perhaps if someone had given LaMotta the power to freeze-frame his life on that day, he would have grabbed at the chance.

"It was bedlam, of course," LaMotta said in his description of the scene at Briggs Stadium, "but the kind of bedlam you want to last forever. What I had now was the gold and jewel-studded championship belt that Joe Louis presented to me, the belt I'd waited all my life for, and the crowd all slapping me on the back and telling me what a great guy I was." [15]

These weren't just any Joes from the cheap seats, either. LaMotta took note as judges, senators, and rich guys paid homage, accompanied by babes wearing slinky low-cut evening gowns. He was the man of the hour—the toast of the boxing world. And he didn't short-change Vikki, either, saying she looked splendid in a dynamite dress.

Then, the strangest thing happened. Of all the places at all the most discordant of times, peering through the crowd surrounding him was someone LaMotta recognized, someone from his distant past. He couldn't even quite identify the man at first. True realization brought shock. Everyone adjourned to LaMotta's hotel for a party, where naturally, he was the center of attention, feted and toasted with champagne. Suddenly, standing there, just a few feet away from him, now talking to him, was a ghost.

Harry Gordon, the bookie he had killed, was right there congratulating him.

14

The Champ

There was no mystery about what Jake LaMotta's next move in the ring would be. As part of the deal he signed to get his chance at the middleweight title, he had to guarantee a rematch to Marcel Cerdan. In this case, it was warranted, anyway. Cerdan fought most of the bout with an injured shoulder. LaMotta fought most of the bout with an injured hand. Still, it had been an exciting and action-packed fight. It would not be difficult for promoters to sell a rematch to boxing fans.

Almost as soon as LaMotta's hand was raised in victory, the debate over where and when the rematch should be held broke out. Detroit seemed like a good place. Hadn't the Motor City supported the first fight? New York City was suggested, too. September was floated as a possible time.

Of course, both men would need time to heal. But during an era when boxers fought much more frequently than they do in the 2000s, nobody thought September was too soon. LaMotta–Cerdan II was scheduled for Madison Square Garden on September 28, and the contract for the rematch was signed by Cerdan before he even left the country.

"I go home in about two weeks," he said. "But then I come back here." [1]

Meanwhile, LaMotta was the new king of Broadway more or less. He was a New Yorker who was now the champion of the world—a youthful dream fulfilled.

However, he was mentally plagued by his shocking encounter with Harry Gordon, a man whom long ago he thought he had murdered. He had been carrying that guilt around for years, and now the man showed up in the flesh.

When LaMotta first realized the man from the neighborhood he had assaulted and left for dead was talking to him after the Cerdan fight, he was in disbelief. His own account of the meeting indicates he was stumbling over his words, baffled, and nearly gave away too much information to someone who had no idea who had done the deed to him.

Two guys muscled through the crowd to offer good wishes. One of them whom LaMotta noted had "a crisscross of ugly, livid scars on his forehead,"[2] said hello, using his old nickname for Jake of "Jakela." LaMotta did not recognize the man at first. Then, he reacted as if seeing a ghost, because in essence he was. It was Harry Gordon, come to pay respects to the new champ. "Jesus. Jesus Christ. Holy Mother of God—Harry Gordon. Harry Gordon! The book," Jake said.[3]

Gordon turned to his partner and basically said, "See, I told you LaMotta would remember me from the neighborhood," because he had been a well-known bookie. Oh my, how LaMotta remembered him, but not because of that. At first, LaMotta was speechless. Then, without thinking but secure in the background knowledge that Harry had made news by being killed, Jake said, "Harry... Harry, you're dead. You're dead, you son of a bitch. I saw it in the paper myself! You're dead!"[4]

Admittedly, that was a strong reaction from a casual acquaintance, especially one who was only a teenager at the time, but at least LaMotta did not say anything incriminating. Gordon just burst out laughing and reassured LaMotta that he was indeed alive, and by the way, how about a glass of champagne for him and his friend in the midst of the celebration.

Gordon then ran through the incident. He said he would have given whoever assaulted him whatever money he was carrying, and that the robber botched the whole thing anyway by missing out on the $1,700 he had hidden. Gordon told LaMotta the newspapers got the story wrong in one important detail. Yes, he had been assaulted. Yes, the thief missed the bucks. But no, he did not die. Everyone in his extended family and everyone in the neighborhood read that and figured old Harry was kaput.

"They printed I was dead instead of only dying," Gordon said. "There was even telegrams sent out to the relatives and friends. They come to sit Shiva [the Jewish mourning ritual], but I fooled them all. And I bet some of them weren't too happy." [5]

Gordon said he spent six weeks in the hospital "one step from the morgue," but when released he went to Florida to live and thus was never seen in the Bronx again. On the heels of the newspaper story, lots of people thought Gordon had died. LaMotta reeled as he heard this tale, and the punch line was even more ironic. Harry Gordon had become a big fan of Jake LaMotta as he worked his way through the ranks as a boxer, and for him, it was must-see theatre to see old Jakela from back home win the world middleweight title.

LaMotta was almost sick over this revelation. He was stunned and overwhelmed. To a degree, he was being absolved of his greatest sin. He had still committed violent assault amid a robbery. But for all his faults, at least LaMotta knew he was no murderer. While he was relieved he hadn't killed the man, he had flashbacks about the night, hitting Gordon with the pipe, trying to steal his money, which all piled immediately upon the emotions of winning the championship. Jake was one confused man for a little while. It wasn't as if LaMotta's conscience should have been clear because he only nearly killed a man, but at least he hadn't killed him. Thus, it wasn't as if all his guilt feelings were misspent over the years.

For the moment, there was every reason to party. LaMotta was treated like royalty in New York. Joey ran around telling everyone his brother was king of the world. For the first time in a long time, LaMotta did not have to fill up his dance card with a series of less-important bouts in a variety of cities.

Next up was Cerdan again, and when he returned to the gym to train, that's what his focus would be on. The goal was to keep the title belt and wear it for as long as he could. He had no intention of being one-and-done the way Cerdan had been. Of course, losing had not entered Cerdan's mind when he arrived in Detroit to face LaMotta. He was hungry to win the middleweight crown back, but he also wanted to return to France for a bit before resuming training for a second crack at LaMotta.

"It is the greatest disappointment in my career," Cerdan said after the loss. "I shall come back in August, fight LaMotta again for the title, and it may be my last fight. It will be a case of do or die and I know I'll regain the crown." [6]

That's the way every fighter thinks or else he would not show up for the bout. Usually, if a fighter loses to an opponent and gets a second chance, he will say he has learned from his mistakes and can apply the lessons to victory a second time around. The result of the first Cerdan–LaMotta fight was somewhat muddied because of their respective injuries. Yet, some believed LaMotta dominated in sufficient fashion to show he would have won no matter what.

Rather than being the charging bull he usually was, LaMotta did pick away at Cerdan more from a distance after he injured his hand and saw he could do damage and pile up points in that manner. "Well, when I hurt my left I found I couldn't punch with it," LaMotta said. "But I could molest Cerdan by poking it in his face. Soon I saw I could do it easily, so I kept it up."[7]

Certainly, if LaMotta came into the first bout loaded with confidence, there was nothing he saw from Cerdan that would diminish that feeling for a rematch.

Although Cerdan insisted he injured his shoulder in the first round, some writers pointed out that he scored so well in the second and third rounds, so couldn't it have happened later?

"I'm sure it happened then," Cerdan said of the first round, speaking in French, "because I felt pain in the second round and tried to use my left, but found it difficult. In the succeeding rounds I couldn't raise my arm."[8]

Shortly after the party wound down in the Bronx feting LaMotta and his feat, he fell into a depression. He was once again haunted by Harry Gordon and the Billy Fox fix. There was nothing he could do to turn back the clock, but beyond the euphoria of the moment, he was so tortured he didn't get as much enjoyment out of being champ as he might have.

Once the cheering stopped, he had plenty of time to think and some of those thoughts were dark ones, even if Vikki did not always know the reasons behind his moods until much later.

"I'm the champ," LaMotta said after his victory, "but look what I had to do to get it," referring to the Fox debacle.[9]

"It was a dirty championship because of the Billy Fox fight," Vikki said years later. "I honestly believe Jake felt inside that once he was champion the sun would shine every day, he'd be happy all the time and life would be perfect.

But the world doesn't work that way, and having won the title he was still depressed without knowing why." [10]

It was always best for Jake to be training for a fight, to have a goal in the ring. The approaching date of a rematch with Cerdan should have been an elixir. This guy had the nerve to want to take his title back. LaMotta couldn't let that happen.

Cerdan was highly motivated. He had his brief taste of glory after lifting the middleweight crown from Tony Zale, and he wanted another taste. The rematch was headed for Madison Square Garden and arena officials assigned Murray Goodman to work as a public relations agent for Cerdan to build him up before the bout. Goodman, a wily and entertaining PR guy who later worked for promoter Don King, was around the fight game for a long time.

Goodman first got to know Cerdan in 1948 before the Zale fight, and he was appalled upon first meeting him to see him sitting around wearing a sling on one arm. Goodman asked what the heck was going on. Cerdan informed him it was really a nothing injury—he had been stung by a bee. Goodman did not want Cerdan to be seen wearing bandages, so he hustled him into the house.

When the LaMotta rematch was agreed to, Goodman rejoined Cerdan's side for his preparations. Only before the September 28, 1949, fight could come off, LaMotta suffered a minor injury that resulted in a postponement. Goodman had watched Cerdan work himself into tip-top shape and knew he was peaking for that date.

Harry Markson, who then ran Madison Square Garden, telephoned Goodman at Cerdan's training camp to let him know about LaMotta's situation.

"LaMotta says he's got a pain in the neck, the fight's off," Markson said." [11]

According to Goodman, who told the story to Hall of Fame boxing writer Jerry Izenberg, Markson left it to him on how to break the word to the challenger.

"I didn't know how to tell him," Goodman relayed. "So I walked up to him and he was sitting in one of the lawn chairs and I simply said call off the workout. LaMotta's supposed to be sick." [12]

An unhappy Cerdan paused in silence for quite some time, and then asked Goodman if he drank whiskey.

"Come, Murray, we drink," Cerdan said.[13]

Goodman said they drank from 3 p.m. one afternoon to 6 a.m. the next morning, and Cerdan not only held his liquor like a champ, he seemed sober when Goodman departed.

The bout was rescheduled for December 2, and the plan was for Goodman to reconvene with Cerdan when he set up training camp once more. Training was disrupted for a while as Cerdan headed back to France. Although he probably did not need to arrive back in the United States quite so early, Cerdan chose to fly out of France on October 27, 1949.

For one thing, his beloved mistress, Edith Piaf, was singing in the United States, at that moment in New York, and he could spend some time with her before going cold turkey into training seclusion. Jo Longman, Cerdan's manager, accompanied him on the return trip.

The flight from Paris–Orly airport to New York City was on an Air France plane with a scheduled stop at Santa Maria Airport in the Azores, an independent portion of Portugal. However, the plane crashed into a mountain on San Miguel Island. There were 48 people aboard, 37 of them passengers and 11 of them crew members, and all perished. Technically, Cerdan's death was on October 28 because the plane crashed at almost 3 a.m. European Central Time.

When Piaf got word her lover had died on his way to see her, she blamed herself for his death. The timing of the plane trip was built around a visit to her, not so much for the LaMotta fight. She was grief-stricken, almost incapable of functioning for some time afterwards.

A biography of Piaf that was quoted on a website about grief, heartbreakingly and poignantly illustrated Piaf's reaction when she received the news of Cerdan's death while in New York playing a nightclub called The Versailles. Although the reality was that there were no survivors and most people understood that, initially some hoped the crash had not killed all aboard and prayers were offered in many quarters.

Piaf was a night owl, a night performer, who slept late. When she emerged from her bedroom on that late October day several of her friends were milling about. She thought Cerdan had arrived and was playing a joke or a game with her by hiding. A friend said, "Edith, you must be brave. There are no survivors." [14]

When the enormity of the truth penetrated her mind, Piaf became hysterical and spent the entire afternoon in tears. Her manager sent word to The Versailles that she could not go on that night. The nightclub boss visited her at her place, and she changed her mind. At first, Piaf did not realize the knowledge of the plane crash was widespread. Journalists attempted to gain insight from her, but all she said was uttered to a photographer, "Oh, Marcel." [15]

In the old tradition of show business, the show did go on. On the way to the nightclub, Piaf had her ride detour to a church, where she lighted a candle for Cerdan in the bitter and vain hope that he was still alive.

Piaf announced to the spectators who filled the club, "Tonight, I am singing for Marcel Cerdan." [16] She somehow made it through the entire show except for the final line of her final song, when she collapsed.

When word reached Jake LaMotta that Marcel Cerdan died in a plane crash on his way to their rematch, the New York fighter, too, at first held out hope for Cerdan's survival. "My mother has been praying. . . lighting candles for the safety of our friend," LaMotta said. "You had to fight him as I did to know what a fine sportsman he was." [17]

After the crash site in the Azores was investigated, Cerdan's remains were returned to France. When the plane landed, the removal of the coffin was filmed. He then lay in state in a Catholic church as thousands of members of the public filed past paying tribute. Then a long motorcade of vehicles bursting with flowers, with many mourners following slowly on foot, wove through the streets. Some say 45,000 people attended the funeral, others 100,000.

Cerdan was buried in Perpignan, Lanquedoc-Rousillon, France. At the very visible grave site sits a sign reading (in French) that the location is an homage to Cerdan. Nearby is a sculpture of a white boxing glove. In 1969, the United Arab Emirates featured Cerdan on a postage stamp. Twice, in 1991 and in 2004, the one-time world middleweight champion was pictured on postage stamps produced in France.

The tragic death of Cerdan prevented a rematch with LaMotta. The New Yorker embarked on his own reign as champion, starting with a search for the next suitable opponent.

One thing LaMotta's conquest of Cerdan in their only fight did for him was to raise his profile worldwide, making him better known in cities beyond New York and Detroit. In October 1949, when LaMotta was the reigning champ and still awaiting that second bout with Cerdan, he graced the cover of *The Ring* magazine.

It was a marvelous looking art-work depiction of LaMotta, illustrating him as a hard man to beat in the ring, with the only words besides the title of the magazine reading, "Jake LaMotta, The Bronx Bull." Looming over LaMotta's left shoulder is a gigantic bull. It was classic kitsch.

15

Being Champion of the World

Jake LaMotta's immediate future had been written in clear contract language. His first bout after winning the middleweight crown from Marcel Cerdan obligated him to fight Cerdan again in a rematch to give the ex-champ a chance to win back his title. Only now there was no more Marcel Cerdan on the scene. LaMotta had been training and wanted to keep active in the ring. Cerdan's death threw the situation into disarray, but LaMotta had to fight to stay sharp. He had suffered a long time for his art, sweating and laboring for years to get the opportunity to fight for the 160-pound title. He wanted to hang onto it for a while.

If his wife, Vikki, is to be listened to, LaMotta was no gracious winner once he owned the belt. All Jake really wanted out of life was to win a world boxing championship. It was his life's ambition, and he made it. He began living too large in embracing the cliché of "to the victor go the spoils."

Boxers are human. Just like World Series champion baseball players, Super Bowl–winning football players, and Olympic gold medalists, they want to celebrate their triumphs. Any athlete can go too far in getting away from the things that carried them to the top, but in no sport is it any more risky than in boxing. Once you let your weight go, you must live through the ordeal of losing extra poundage to fit into your weight class again.

Boxing is unforgiving. There are always younger guys coming along who want to knock your block off. A fighter must be mentally and physically honed to be at his best. Jake was never good at staying at a prime fighting weight. If anything, once he won the 160-pound crown, it was easier to eat and drink his way up to 175 or 180 pounds. He convinced himself that he had always lost the weight before, so it would come off again this time.

"More and more he [LaMotta] sought to bolster his ego by being loud and obnoxious," Vikki said. "'Have no fear, the champ is here,' he'd tell people. If I disagreed with him about anything, all I heard was, 'Don't answer the champ back. Nobody talks back to the champ.'" [1]

A tell-tale sign someone's ego has grown larger than the planet Venus is when they begin talking about themselves in the third person.

Vikki was amazed to watch her husband get caught up in all the hype of being a champion while at the same time forgetting how he became a champion. Vikki said she didn't drink, usually only imbibing Coca-Cola with cherries on top. As Jake battled his way to the title, he was an abstainer, too. No more, she said. Everyone wanted to hang around with the champ. Everyone wanted to treat him to a drink. Everyone wanted to share the night with a world boxing titlist.

"Well, he was the champ," she said. "Why not have a drink? And then another. Which is death for a fighter. Soon, he was losing the motivation to train. 'I'm not doing road work today. Instead of running, I'll spar an extra round in the gym.' He wasn't hungry anymore. The edge was gone." [2]

The way Vikki describes this period of her marriage to Jake sounds like it was the worst of times instead of what should have been the best of times. When someone pursues a goal for so long, he should feel pleased and satisfied that he has accomplished something special. But it was Cerdan's life that ended after the title fight, not LaMotta's. It was almost as if he wanted to stop time and just be the champion without bothering to perform as the champion in the ring.

Sooner or later, a fighter that is not retired must fight. Sooner or later, a champion must defend his crown or else it will be stripped from him. No one could have blamed LaMotta if there was a little voice in his head urging him to take it easy, have a good time, make up for all the hardships and everything he had been put through before taking on a fresh challenge.

But LaMotta was in no position to freeze the title and just do nothing. In Vikki's view, LaMotta's career was still being guided by the mob in the sense that gangsters were picking his opponents. Although not unaware of the pressures on LaMotta, from her standpoint Jake was practically half out of his mind about everything, especially his jealousy over her. It was unceasing and demanding to extremes beyond belief. He even was jealous when her brother stayed over-night while he was out of town, acting as a protector so she wouldn't have to stay alone.

In her mind, LaMotta was never secure in her love. Once when he was at a training camp, LaMotta sneaked home because his brother told him she was cheating with another guy—he had heard him talking in the background while she was on the phone. The other guy? She had been talking to Jake! They had been lovey-dovey on the telephone. Jake was his own mystery man.

As the years passed, LaMotta was a tormented soul, deep down believing everything in his life would be okay when he won the championship. He was incapable of seeing the good in his daily life—a wife and children who loved him. LaMotta was always fixated on being deprived of a title shot. When LaMotta became champ, the debacle with Fox loomed over his head. Not every sportswriter was his pal—many did not like him and he didn't like them as a group. Worse than the sportswriters' own words were the headlines copy editors placed above the articles. It stuck in Vikki's mind for years that some papers and magazines referred to Jake as the "most hated man in boxing."

LaMotta had never gone out of his way to make friends and indeed had become attached to the mob, but using the word *hate* was pretty strong and a bit sensational. Still, to some, that was middleweight champ Jake LaMotta's image.

During that time when boxers often fought every few weeks, champions did get a break and avoid defenses for a few months at a time. What was common, however, was signing to fight nontitle bouts, something that never occurs today. These days, if a champion fights, it is a championship bout. In Jake's day, a fighter could take a bout for a payday or the workout and not worry about surrendering the belt.

It was a good thing, too. After Cerdan died in the plane crash, thus obviously eliminating the rematch from the schedule, LaMotta agreed to instead fight Robert Villemain at Madison Square Garden on December 12, 1949. LaMotta had already met Villemain. Earlier in the year on March 25, as a lead-up fight to the title bout with Cerdan, LaMotta had captured a split decision.

That fight was close enough that scheduling a rematch, for the entertainment value if nothing else since the title was not at stake, made it a saleable confrontation for the public. Also, Villemain, like Cerdan, was of French extraction. He was born in Paris in 1924. All things examined, there should have been enough evidence to show LaMotta he needed to show up in shape and he could not coast. Given the backdrop of Vikki's comments about Jake skimping on training, keeping late hours, and drinking alcohol, it did not seem as if LaMotta took this bout very seriously.

That lackadaisical behavior cost LaMotta. Even he later admitted he had lost his edge after achieving his ambition. He also felt lighter with the knowledge that he had not been a murderer: had not killed Harry Gordon. He had loathed himself for that act, and while what he did was the act of a reckless punk, he had not committed murder.

"The drive had gone out of me," he said, "and worst of all I was beginning to get bored by it all. But I was still going to remain champion for as long as I could. I felt that if I had to I could always push the right buttons and become as vicious and mean as I had to be. I had been conditioned too long and too hard to suddenly lose that. But it just wasn't the same as being a mean, cruel bastard every minute of the day just because you believed yourself to be." [3]

Villemain was no slouch. His lifetime record was 52-7-4, and he even had a passing physical resemblance to Cerdan, though he never won a title and was never viewed as a romantic figure in France. At one point, Villemain owned the Pennsylvania middleweight title, of all things. Amongst his victims in his busy career between 1944 and 1952 was Hall of Famer Kid Gavilán. Villemain also defeated Laurent Dauthuille (twice), who had given LaMotta so much trouble.

It was a good thing for LaMotta there was no belt up for grabs in the 1949 fight because Villemain won by unanimous decision. "I admit I looked terrible losing to Villemain," LaMotta said, "and there was a lot of talk that I was ready to be taken." [4]

There was wryness in LaMotta's tone when suddenly a large group of middleweights began clamoring for a shot at the title. One look at an out-of-sorts LaMotta in the ring against Villemain and everyone wanted to fight him. They all thought they could punch out an apparently over-the-hill Jake and swipe the belt.

LaMotta knew he had let his conditioning go and had piled up enough weight that he was a better fit at light-heavyweight than at middleweight. But he did not mentally hold himself accountable. His attitude was more like, "What do you expect?" Meaning that after training hard for the biggest fight of his career, he deserved to blow off steam partying.

The strategy LaMotta devised to get himself back in trim was signing to fight nontitle light-heavyweight bouts and gradually lose his excess poundage before making a middleweight title defense, which is what he did. After the Christmas and New Year's holidays, LaMotta faced Dick Wagner on February 3, 1950, at his old standby home, the Detroit Olympia.

Wagner was a tough guy born in Washington state with a lifetime record of 34-20-5. He was hard to knock out, but was not quite a top-tier fighter. By the time Wagner met LaMotta, he had already faced the infamous Billy Fox and beat him twice. The last two bouts of Wagner's career later were against heavyweight champion Floyd Patterson when young Patterson was on his way up the ladder in 1953. As fine a boxer as Patterson was, Wagner gave him difficult tussles. Floyd prevailed by a technical knockout and split decision. LaMotta also stopped Wagner by technical knockout.

Another sturdy fighter who got off to a great start, but became an opponent who just could not get past the best fighters of the day, was Chuck Hunter of Cleveland. Hunter won a lot but not against the big-name guys. LaMotta, also popular in Cleveland, had no qualms about taking on Hunter in his hometown. When they met on February 28, 1950, Hunter may have harbored hopes of reviving his career.

At one point, Hunter was 17-3. He ended up 46-25-1. Some of those losses were to such luminaries as Rocky Graziano, Bobo Olson, Harold Johnson, Tommy Yarosz, and yes, Jake LaMotta on that night at the arena in Cleveland by technical knockout.

The last a trio of these light-heavy tune-ups was against Joe Taylor of Binghamton, New York, in nearby Syracuse at the State Fair Coliseum. Taylor did not fight as many big names as Hunter, though he did split with Joey DeJohn, en route to a 36-15-2 mark. LaMotta out-worked Taylor for a unanimous decision.

LaMotta's next fight would be his first defense of the middleweight crown he lifted from Cerdan. It was scheduled for July 12, 1950, against Tiberio Mitri at Madison Square Garden. It had been more than a year since LaMotta bested Cerdan to capture the belt. He liked the way the bauble fit, and he wanted to keep wearing it.

Born in Trieste, Italy, in 1926, Mitri went 50-0 at the start of his career. He won the Italian and European middleweight championships. Nicknamed "The Trieste Tiger," Mitri piled up an 88-7-6 professional record between 1946 and 1957. Mitri also defeated Dick Wagner in one of his rare U.S. fights leading up to the LaMotta opportunity. Mostly, he fought in Italy, but he made appearances in Switzerland, Australia, Tunisia, England, France, and Belgium. Later, he became a movie actor in Italy.

It was not clear if Mitri would ever have received a shot at the world championship, however, but for one good break. LaMotta was all set to meet his old friend, Rocky Graziano, in this title defense, but Graziano had to pull out. It was the closest the two old acquaintances from the streets of New York and Coxsackie prison came to blows with a championship belt and a purse to be awarded.

LaMotta looked at a Graziano fight as a big money-maker, one that would divide allegiances all around New York. It was going to be a bigger hit than any other theatre in New York, and that year *Guys and Dolls*, *Brigadoon*, and *Carousel* were playing. It did have potential to be an all-time classic fight. There was a lot of talk about another Sugar Ray

Robinson bout, this time for a title, but LaMotta lobbied for Graziano first.

"The minute I even mentioned a Graziano fight, all I got was static," LaMotta said, "first of all, from Rocky, of all people. I couldn't figure him out." LaMotta said Graziano, who was admittedly viewed as a goofball in some quarters, had said at the time, "'I don't want no title. I had too much trouble when I had it.' But I was convinced that a LaMotta-Graziano fight would be a natural and also would make a fortune. This would be a real fight." [5]

It almost happened. A deal was signed, the hype began, but only days into workouts the fight was called off because Graziano broke his hand in training. That was the end of that. Many years later, appearing on a televised boxing talk show, LaMotta was asked who would have won between him and Graziano.

"It would have been a rough bout," LaMotta said. "I would have licked him." [6]

At that stage of both of their careers, LaMotta was probably right. He also was almost certainly correct in believing that a LaMotta–Graziano fight would have drawn a much larger gate than a LaMotta–Mitri fight. In the case of Mitri, it was pretty much "Who's he?" in the local papers, never mind amongst fight fans.

Still, it counted as the long-awaited first LaMotta title defense.

16

Defending the Title

On July 12, 1950, Jake LaMotta entered a boxing ring for the first time introduced as the middleweight champion of the world. Gazing across the ring, he saw that era's Italian Stallion, Tiberio Mitri, the man who wanted to take away his hard-earned title.

There was no question that the crowd in Madison Square Garden was for Jake. He was the hometown guy. Oh, there was plenty of support for Italians in New York City, from Joe DiMaggio in center field for the Yankees, to Jake's pal Rocky Graziano in the boxing world, to Mama Leone's famous restaurant.

However, the New York fans didn't know Mitri. He was just a name from Europe. LaMotta was their Italian, the one from the Bronx who always provided so much excitement. LaMotta had lost some of his support in the wake of the Billy Fox fight and the authorities' investigation. But except for the Fox fight, he always delivered when the bell rang. He gave the customer a show for his money.

Mitri was surprisingly good based on how little was really known about his skills. He was one of those sleeper fighters. None of the in-the-know guys knew a lot about Mitri despite his 50-0 record. He mostly fought far, far away against opponents they knew even less about. The scouting report for LaMotta to study was limited. There were no films of Mitri's fights to learn from.

Jake could have used the help. If anyone thought Mitri was going to be a pushover and that LaMotta would knock him out early, the reality was quite different. Mitri could fight and was a threat to LaMotta, if only staying around for all 15 rounds. When a bout goes the distance, it means the judges are in charge, and they get to vote. The opportunity for a boxer to finish things without mathematical assistance has passed.

Mitri stuck around for fifteen rounds, an entire 45 minutes of mayhem. LaMotta was his usual bullish self and did not wilt, but neither could he polish off Mitri. In the end, he prevailed by unanimous decision. Would a younger Jake have disposed of Mitri more readily? Would a Jake who hadn't been sampling the night life taken care of business more efficiently?

These were open questions, but they were not asked from the standpoint of defeat. If you don't have the best night of your career and you still walk away with a victory, then you are playing with house money. Perhaps you feel lucky or relief. Perhaps you learn a lesson.

Before the fight, LaMotta was told Mitri fought like Marcel Cerdan. Afterwards, he had a different opinion. One way Mitri survived the 15 rounds with Jake was his style. Fans always underestimate the contrast in personal styles between boxers, which has nothing to do with their overall records. Some fighters are just bad matchups. That's how LaMotta saw Mitri after spending so much time with him in close quarters inside the ring.

"He would get off balance," LaMotta said, "and one thing a top fighter rarely is, is off balance." Mitri's methods threw Jake off-balance in terms of trying to catch up with him for clean shots. This made Mitri hard to finish off, LaMotta said, "largely because it's hard to fight that kind of fighter and I was piling up points so fast, why should I risk busting a hand on his head trying to nail him?"[1]

Maybe that was an excuse for not taking Mitri out, or maybe that was the literal truth.

The key was that LaMotta was still champ and looking for his next challenger. Actually, the gangsters whom Jake sold his soul to with the Billy Fox fix and the groomed pathway to the title fight were still running things, pretty much telling him whom he had to defend against. They chose an interesting opponent.

For LaMotta's second middleweight title defense, the foe was Laurent Dauthuille, back by popular demand. Well, maybe, maybe not, but a credible opponent. The men did have their history. While Dauthuille is not well-remembered now, he was an excellent fighter. In 1949, he had won a unanimous decision over LaMotta, so no one could say LaMotta was fighting a bum.

Leading up to the September 13, 1950, title match, Dauthuille had a four-fight winning streak going and had won 10 out of his last 11 fights. His only loss between December 1948 and the title fight came to Kid Gavilan. No boxer was ever embarrassed to have a loss to Kid Gavilan on his résumé.

Born in Cuba, Gavilan won the world welterweight title and put together a record of 108-30-5, including wins over Ike Williams, Johnny Bratton, Carmen Basilio, Chuck Davey, Beau Jack, and Billy Graham. Active between 1943 and 1958, "The Cuban Hawk" became a Hall of Fame fighter. Gavilan fought the best and beat the best.

Dauthuille made Gavilan go the distance, but lost a unanimous decision against him in Montreal in November 1949, 10 months before Dauthuille bested LaMotta. It should be observed, though, that Dauthuille had twice lost to Robert Villemain. One thing France had going for it during this boxing era was a surfeit of quality middleweights. Now Dauthuille and Jake were pitted again for the most important bout of Dauthuille's career. Since it was about holding on to the title, it might be said this was also the most important bout of LaMotta's career. Indeed, once the title was in his possession, each successive championship bout was the most important fight of his career as he scratched and clawed to hold onto the belt.

Dauthuille had all the tools to lift LaMotta's crown, so it never figured to be an easy bout. It seemed as if LaMotta had few of those anymore, but this one was tougher than most. It was held at the Olympia in Detroit once more, one of LaMotta's favorite venues. LaMotta came in a 3-1 favorite and attendance was 11,426.

Not everyone close to Jake thought he should be favored. Like Vikki, his brother Joey noted how LaMotta sloughed off in training, ate too much, stayed out too late, and hadn't prepared with the same tenacity he had in the past. The two men had an argument leading up to the Dauthuille fight with Joey saying Jake should pull out and not fight again until he was really ready. Jake related their verbal exchange in *Raging Bull.*

"The trouble is, you get through a fight, you chase around too much, you eat too much of that pasta, you drink too much booze," Joey accused his brother. "I ain't fightin' for the title! Go ahead and blow it! See if I care! Aw, what the hell's the use, you're gonna blow it to somebody sometime, anyway. What the hell has gotten into you? You're not the same fighter you used to be." [2]

Jake became enraged after digesting these taunts.

"Whaddaya mean I'm not the same fighter I was?" he responded.

"You got no zing," Joey answered back, citing sloppy training. [3]

For the first dozen rounds, it seemed the boxing fans that took the bet at those odds were suckers. A lot of the talk leading up to the bout was that LaMotta was showing signs of age and deterioration in the ring, and he might be ripe to be taken. He did start slowly, and Dauthuille seemed to be the fighter with all the pep. He threw stinging jabs, demonstrated ring generalship, and was prepped for LaMotta's style. When Jake tried to lay back to lure Dauthuille in close, the challenger did not bite.

As the rounds ticked by, the big picture wasn't pretty. Jake was being out-boxed and outfoxed, falling behind on all the judges' scorecards. He wasn't getting to Dauthuille for good shots, and the challenger evaded many of Jake's body shots, which were normally his bread and butter.

LaMotta was flat. Dauthuille hit him enough to draw blood from above LaMotta's left eye, and Jake did not have his usual snap, nor did he deliver the way he usually did when getting close enough inside to pepper his foe with body blows. Early on, LaMotta also injured his right thumb, which made it harder to throw good punches.

Some fighters are always dangerous, even if they appear drained and out of contention. Sometimes because they possess big thunder in their fists, they have the potential for a knockout blow at any time. That means they are never out of it. It's like drawing upon a three-run homer in the ninth inning to pull out a baseball game that looked hopeless. The phrase "a puncher's chance" applies here. But, Jake was not a big puncher. He did not have that one-punch knockout power in his repertoire.

As the rounds passed and Dauthuille was having his way with the middleweight title genuinely in his sights, there seemed little LaMotta could do to salvage the situation. Again, in baseball terms, he needed a rally not capped by one big swing, but a pieced-together rally where the little things paid off.

The rounds clicked by. The bell rang every three minutes, and the fighters rested on their stools. The bell rang again, and they met in mid-ring to resume their assaults. There was no dispute which way the wind was blowing. The points piled up for the challenger. LaMotta's performance did not pass the eye test. Keeping track in one's head was one thing, but just looking at what was going on before their very eyes the Detroit fans knew LaMotta was in serious jeopardy.

Over and over Dauthuille scored. He flicked his jab, he landed rights, he mixed up his punches. LaMotta was not a zombie, but he was missing his usual zest and could not strategize to keep away from Dauthuille's best punches. One magazine (borrowing from another) reported that LaMotta "worked like a man in a daze." [4]

In the old days when title fights were scheduled for 15 rounds, it was said rounds 13, 14, and 15 separated the men from the boys, the contenders from the pretenders. Those final three rounds were called the championship rounds because they revealed character and what it truly took to be the best. Yet, even in rounds 13 and 14, LaMotta could not press his case. He certainly seemed headed for defeat and being forced to hand over the championship belt to Dauthuille.

Anyone who sees enough boxing knows that in a circumstance like this, the fighter in the lead should employ a very conservative strategy for the 15th round—just stay on your feet and parry all forays from the desperate opponent. Make no mistake about it, Jake was desperate as the 15th round began.

When it was over, there was considerable debate and curiosity about what took place in Dauthuille's corner during the one-minute rest period before the 15th round began. Corners can be chaotic with excited seconds, trainers, managers, and those closest to the fighter exhorting him onward as the clock ticks down. Their man was "this" close to winning the world championship, so why shouldn't Dauthuille's helpers be excited?

But what did they tell him above the noise of the buzzing crowd? Only one instruction made sense—to stay away from LaMotta's strength, to fight conservatively even if you lose the round, because you don't need the round to win. Hymie Blaustein, one of Dauthuille's corner men, did his best to annunciate that clear-headed, common-sense message to the fighter.

"Stay away and box," Blaustein said. "Easy, easy. You have the title." [5]

Although there is no way to know in the corner what the official scores are on judges' closely held scoresheets, the evidence seemed overwhelmingly in favor of Dauthuille. It came out later that through 14 rounds, the scores for Dauthuille read 72-68, 74-66, and 73-67; not even close. Dauthuille was waltzing away with LaMotta's crown.

Not everyone in the crowded corner, though, saw things through either the judges' or Blaustein's eyes. Others felt Dauthuille could not play it safe. Over the years, judges have been known to be kinder than necessary to incumbents. There is sometimes a subliminal belief that a challenger must do more in combat to wrest the title than the champion does to keep it. Someone told Dauthuille to go after LaMotta, to take it to him to ensure he could win on points. And that's what he did.

Rather than stay in the middle of the ring and dodge LaMotta's pressure at the beginning of the 15th round, Dauthuille maneuvered into Jake's corner. This was not all bad at first because Dauthuille got in his licks, connecting with a left-right combination to LaMotta's jaw. The men stood toe-to-toe exchanging good scoring blows. But,

Dauthuille had no business doing that because there was no need. Dauthuille was not unscathed. He took enough punishment to be marked around both eyes.

Dauthuille had to be pleased, however, because he was landing more and better punches than LaMotta, in his own mind sealing the champ's defeat. Until suddenly, he wasn't anymore. Now it was LaMotta's turn. He threw a big left that landed flush, then followed it up with a short hard right to the jaw that stopped Dauthuille in his tracks. Dauthuille nearly dropped from the shot. People say his knees buckled from the punch. The starch had been taken out of Dauthuille. One minute he was fighting for glory, the next for survival.

After that brief onslaught, Dauthuille was not fighting back, but was on the move trying to escape LaMotta's fists. He slid along the ropes trying to get away from him. The challenger could not escape. For Dauthuille, it was like being trapped in a corral.

"When he dropped his hands in my corner, I knew I had him," LaMotta said afterwards.[6]

LaMotta was like a shark smelling blood, going in for the kill. He had Dauthuille trapped, nearly wide open to his attack, and the punches rained down, lefts and rights both, switching between blows to the head and blows to the belly—many punches to the body. The accumulation of punches took its toll, and LaMotta knocked Dauthuille down and almost through the ropes. The challenger lay on his back across the bottom rope.

Referee Lou Handler's count began, and he did not stop counting until he reached 10—done. LaMotta was the winner by knockout with just 13 seconds left in the final round. If Dauthuille could have somehow pushed himself to his feet in less than 10 seconds, he still would have won the title on points.

In the aftermath, tears were shed and questions were asked in Dauthuille's locker room. Dazed from the ferocity of the finishing attack, Dauthuille was still digesting how things had slipped away in the end.

"I thought I had him for sure," Dauthuille said. "But I guess I got a little bit careless." [7]

Incredibly, LaMotta was still champ. He pretty much only won the last 30 seconds of the fight, but it was enough. Needing a knockout, he got one.

Observers at ringside realized they had watched something remarkable. When the ballots were in at the conclusion of 1950, the Jake LaMotta–Laurent Dauthuille bout was chosen as Fight of the Year. The 15th round, when LaMotta salvaged his title, was selected as Round of the Year.

One view of the drama and action read this way, penned by a sportswriter on the scene in Detroit for the bout: "with only thirty seconds to go [we] felt we just had seen the middleweight title change hands. Thirty seconds left, in a fifteen-round fight which had warmed up into one of the greatest middleweight title struggles in more than a decade." [8]

After he persevered and survived, LaMotta knew Joey had been correct. He had not prepared properly and his lack of energy and pizzazz in the ring nearly cost him. Only his last-round will and desperation kept the title and overcame his preparation mistakes.

17

Sugar Ray Again

After fighting one another five times, Jake LaMotta and Sugar Ray Robinson drifted into separate orbits for a few years. But now with Jake's middleweight title on the line, their epic series of bouts was scheduled to resume. The next contender given a shot at LaMotta was his old nemesis, Robinson.

LaMotta had taken the title from Marcel Cerdan in June 1949 and made two successful defenses. The fight against Robinson was scheduled for February 14, 1951, Valentine's Day, at Chicago Stadium.

Quite a lot had happened in Sugar Ray's life since their last fight on September 26, 1945. Almost five-and-a-half years had gone by—an eternity in a boxer's career.

LaMotta and Robinson had excited the boxing world as few had in any series in the history of the sport through their first five matches. Of course, as dramatic and close as they had been, Robinson won four of them, so after the passage of years some might have suggested it was a low-percentage deal for Jake to take on Sugar Ray again.

Between 1943 and 1951, Robinson won 91 professional fights in a row. As of 1951, his lifetime record was 128 victories, one loss, and four draws with the single loss being to LaMotta. Robinson had ruled the welterweight division with an iron fist, as expected once he got his opportunity to capture the crown. He won the 147-pound class in 1946 and kept that world championship belt until 1951.

For several years early in their careers, LaMotta and Robinson were as linked as another 1940s couple—

Humphrey Bogart and Lauren Bacall—though not in as friendly a manner. In the interim between 1945 and 1951, they had very much lived their own lives that had carried them in different directions, even if they were still amongst the preeminent pugilists in the world.

LaMotta got married to Vikki, had children, dealt with the pressure from the mob, badly handled the fixed fight with Billy Fox, careened through the post-fight investigations, won the middleweight title from Cerdan, lived the high life in celebration, and fought off recent challengers for the crown.

Robinson had been married to Edna Mae, a former dancer at the Cotton Club, since 1943. As Robinson's stature rose and he made good paydays, he invested in style. He inherited his preference for dressy clothes from his father, Walker Smith Sr. He drove a pink Cadillac and everyone in Harlem knew who it belonged to and left it alone. He liked to sing, dance, and hang out with musicians.

By then, Robinson had opened his own Harlem nightclub, too, at 124th Street and 7th Avenue. He was the boss of his own place with his name out front in bright lights. Proprietorship made him proud. If he wanted to see and be seen, party, or just hang out, Robinson could do it in his own establishment. Furthermore, he had a mini-real estate empire with an office for manager George Gainford, a barber shop, and a lingerie shop for his wife. The nightclub was called "Sugar Ray's." What else?

Although Robinson did not have tense relations with mobsters who kept him away from a title, the sport's casual racism of the era did play a role in the politics making it difficult to obtain his title chance. Such was the plight of many top black fighters of the era. Joe Louis seemed to be the exception, a "good Negro" who had proven himself.

Ultimately, Robinson was such a good fighter, he could not be denied his chance.

The welterweight title meeting between Robinson and Tommy Bell was set for Madison Square Garden, a home-town match for Robinson then. The date was December 20, 1946, and at last Robinson, who burned as furiously as LaMotta to have his name placed in the record books, got his shot. By the end of the night, fending Bell off for a unanimous decision, Robinson was crowned the world wel-terweight champion. Like LaMotta, he had been called an uncrowned champ for too long. His belief that he was the best was vindicated in this fight, setting the record straight for history's sake.

This was no gimme fight, however, as fans quickly discovered when Bell's powerful left connected and sent Robinson to the canvas in the second round. The referee counted to seven on the knockdown before Robinson po-sitioned himself to resume the fight.

"My face was on the floor before my ass was," Robinson said of the stunning knockdown. [1]

It took some time for Robinson to recover from the blow. Bell, whose lifetime record was 53-29-3, continued to press him and showed he had no fear of either Sugar Ray's speed or reputation. Bell had whipped himself into the best shape of his life and it was showing.

However, Robinson had guts and staying power. Even after Bell wobbled him again in the fifth round, Robinson shook it off and gained control of the situation. He started to turn things his way in the sixth round and then took over in the later rounds.

Sugar Ray knocked Bell down in the 10th round and nearly ended the fight early with a flurry in the 11th. He was in charge then. When the bell sounded, it became clear Robinson had swayed the judges. He won on points.

"After all those years of being bypassed," Robinson said, "after sixty-three pro fights, at last I was the crowned champion." [2]

Robinson had shirked training because he was anxious to get his club open before the fight five days before Christmas. His hired help just could not make the hoped-for-deadline that quickly. Robinson and his wife drove past the location after he won the crown that night. Some of the workmen were still on site and on the spur-of-the-moment, the couple and the men celebrated with a Coca-Cola toast.

"It was one of the nicest celebrations I ever had," Robinson said. "[3]

Sugar Ray's did open a few days later in time for Christmas of 1946. The Robinsons had a bigger celebration that night.

Between that victory and February 1949, Robinson captured 15 more fights. The most notable victim was Kid Gavilan. Next, he had a draw with Henry Brimm. No one else could touch Robinson during that period before he faced LaMotta. Sugar Ray topped name guys like Bobo Olson and Robert Villemain (twice) and Charley Fusari. He was as great with the title in his hands as he had been beforehand.

However, mixed in with that stretch of successful glory was a horrible, haunting experience. The first four fights after Robinson bested Bell for the crown were non-title fights. Then he signed to fight Jimmy Doyle in Cleveland on June 24, 1947.

Doyle was a tough guy. Born in Los Angeles in 1924, his parents were of Creole heritage from the New Orleans area.

He was 43-6 when he engaged Robinson and tried to claim the welterweight crown. Doyle gave an acceptable accounting of himself that surprised many over the first half of the fight. However, in the eighth round Robinson rallied and landed a picture-perfect lightning left hook. When it landed precisely on Doyle's jaw, the punch knocked him down. Doyle hit his head when he hit the floor, too, and referee Jack Davis stopped the bout before completing the 10-count.

Doyle was carried from the ring on a stretcher and quickly driven to St. Vincent Charity Hospital by a speeding ambulance, where he underwent brain surgery in the middle of the night. Some 17 hours later, Doyle, 22, died from a head injury. Robinson had killed a man in the ring— the worst nightmare for any boxer.

Disturbed by the ultimate result, Robinson said he would fight benefit bouts with the proceeds going to Doyle's family. If Robinson's fighting style was affected by Doyle's death in any major way, it was not apparent. He continued performing as one of the best boxing talents on the planet.

On a much lighter note, it was Robinson, well ahead of Muhammad Ali or any other flashy athlete, who essentially invented the entourage. Boxers, in particular, traveled light. They did not need motor homes to fit the gang in. They hit the road with a manager and a trainer, and occasionally a family member.

Robinson set the tone for the future when an athlete might show up at an event in the company of everyone from a personal cook to a hair dresser, to some relatives and friends, as well as his official seconds. In Robinson's case, his sister, Evelyn, might come along, and he had a secretary. Robinson had hardly been a social animal as a child, but he grew into the role of band leader so to speak, enjoying a crowd around him and providing several of the individuals with jobs. Some people thought Robinson was nuts for doing this, but he had a lot of fun with his people. Later, when a European promoter sought to capitalize on Robinson's fame and set up bouts for him around France, Belgium, Switzerland, Germany, and London, Robinson agreed to make the tour. He had one proviso, however. His pink Cadillac had to come with him for company. The ocean liner freight cost was included in the deal.

When LaMotta began preparing for his sixth fight against Robinson, he had no illusions about the talents of the man he was going to face. He likely knew as much about Robinson as Edna Mae did, though in a different intimate way, knowing whatever physical weak spots he might have.

This was a potential history-making fight. No reigning welterweight champion had ever beaten a reigning middle-weight champion, so if Robinson was victorious, it would be a first. The last time the feat had been attempted was in 1925 when Mickey Walker lost to Harry Greb.

The duo had fought five times, an almost absurd number for two world champions. Each of the five fights had gone the distance. That meant 52 three-minute rounds, slow dancing together. They understood each other's strengths and weaknesses. They should have practically been able to read one another's minds. They were already linked forever in boxing history. Yet, it was true that the one thing lacking in their series was any title being decided by the confrontations. This time the biggest prize in their sport, a world title, would be at issue. This time the winner would receive a very tangible reward besides cash.

In their past bouts with no contract weight really enforced, there was a considerable spread in their weights on fight nights. Robinson was a natural welterweight at 147 pounds, and he only gained a few pounds for some of their matches. LaMotta always had difficulty bringing his weight down to the middleweight limit, although he always made it when the time came. Sometimes, in nontitle bouts, he took on light-heavyweights and seemed just as comfortable in the range of 175 pounds.

It is not uncommon for a fighter to grow into a larger weight class. It was much more difficult in the early 1950s when there were just eight divisions. Now there are junior-this and super-that classes where the weight spread is insignificant, sometimes only three or four pounds at the lightest weights. When LaMotta and Robinson fought, the welterweight limit was 147 pounds and the middleweight limit was 160 pounds.

During their first handful of meetings, LaMotta and Robinson were far apart in weight, sometimes around 15 pounds. That is a big advantage for the heavier man, LaMotta. It may even explain why Robinson was unable to knock Jake out even when dominating in some of their fights.

This time around, it was going to be different. The name of the division was middleweight and the limit was certain, at 160 pounds.

Vikki LaMotta said when her husband signed for the Valentine's Day bout in early January, he weighed 177 pounds. LaMotta said it was actually much worse at 187 pounds. Jake had to lose at least 17 pounds by the weigh-in. She also recalled something peculiar, even almost sinister, going on with Jake shortly after he won the title. She claimed a doctor contacted him and told him he had a substance made from the juices of a bull that was produced in Italy, and it would greatly increase LaMotta's strength if he took the injections. It sounded fanciful, but Vikki said Jake was swayed by the argument that he could become strong like a real bull.

"Right away he was taking the shots," she said. [4]

There is no way of knowing so many years later, and even Jake would probably not know, if those shots were early versions of the steroids that body builders, football players, and baseball players later became so enamored with and are now illicit. Vikki said when she did research, she was told little was known about the ingredients and their effects, but the substance could cause cancer.

Jake had strong reactions to the drugs, and she said she pleaded with him to stop the injections. But, he believed in their promised magical properties. There were good reasons for Vikki to worry. She said Jake's face turned blue, and his feet were icy cold once when he took an overdose. The dosages also made it more difficult for LaMotta to lose the weight he needed to lose.

Vikki said a doctor she checked with told her the drugs were not good for Jake. He gained excessive water weight, but she said when she relayed the doctor's report, Jake brushed her off, saying, "What do you know about boxing? I'm the champ. You mind your own business. I'll take care of the fighting." [5]

Charting the weight loss, when LaMotta accelerated his crash diet of 1,500 calories a day for four weeks, boiling a steak and mixing the juice with water to create a meat soup as a meal, Vikki knew Jake was going to have trouble fooling the scale. She said LaMotta was still at 164+ and four-and-a-half pounds overweight the night before the weigh-in, and he stayed up all night in a steam room to hit the mark.

Jake did it, though. He weighed in at 160 pounds, though likely he was quite weak from the endurance contest of losing the poundage. Robinson, who in the past had trouble gaining weight, weighed in at 155 ½, reasonably close to the middleweight limit and for the first time much closer to

Jake's weight. By that point in his career, however, Robinson had grown into a regular fit in the 153-to-158 range.

While fight fans never seemed to tire of the LaMotta–Robinson matchup, given their history and betting odds of 17½–5 favoring Robinson, not so many gamblers took a put-down-your-money interest in the proceedings.

There had been some insider wondering about LaMotta, who had eschewed gym appearances and sparring for a few days leading up to the bout. He had dropped out of sight and many figured he was focused on losing weight through exercise or steam baths. If LaMotta didn't make 160 pounds, he was going to forfeit his title, so dropping weight had to be his first priority. One sports columnist suggested LaMotta was sitting in his Palmer House hotel room reading *The Basic Writings of Sigmund Freud*.[6]

If so, it was probably a library book on loan since LaMotta never spoke about his favorite reading subjects and probably was as psychologically ready to go as he was going to be without the world-champion shrink's assistance.

The boxers met at the weigh-in at 10 a.m. at Chicago Stadium and exchanged few words, nothing really heated. Despite their familiarity due to frequency of combat, they had nothing specific against one another.

"Well, Jake, this is the sixth time we've met," Robinson said. "This is for the championship. Always we have gave [sic] a good fight. There will be a big crowd here tonight, let's not let them down." LaMotta seemed to have no interest in banter. "Well, boy, you got to be a talker all at once," he said. "We get paid to fight, not to talk."[7]

It was not exactly scintillating repartee, but Jake may have been grumpy due to his starvation diet and was likely in a hurry to get to the refrigerator or a dining table.

In an oddity, two members of the sporting press from France (who perhaps used a somewhat half-baked idea to convince their papers to pay their expenses to send them to Chicago) arrived, informing Robinson he was being viewed as an honorary French citizen for the purpose of avenging Marcel Cerdan against LaMotta. Robinson likely smiled, thanked them for their support, and promptly forgot about what he viewed as a quirky gesture. He had enough to worry about and enough motivation on his own.

Even before the fight, there was some talk that if Robinson won, capturing the title, a seventh bout against LaMotta might be signed to take place within three months of this one. One thing at a time, though.

The bout was scheduled for 15 rounds, but Jake didn't have it in him to go the distance after his long-term starvation program. Robinson was as light on his feet as ever, boxing with his effervescent style. LaMotta, as always, stalked, coming forward relentlessly. For the first eight rounds, Robinson picked away at Jake with ease and piled up points, but as was in his blood, Jake kept on coming.

After the eighth round, Robinson was the boss. He pounded LaMotta mercilessly and ceaselessly, cutting up LaMotta's face, stopping him in his tracks, and pummeling him against the ropes. LaMotta was likely groggy, but he told himself one thing over and over again. He would not be knocked down. At one point, his situation was so precarious he actually wrapped his arm around a rope, nearly knotting it, to hold himself upright.

By then, Vikki did not see nobility, but horror. She said she was screaming and crying, and ultimately praying, "Let it be over. Please! Let it end." [8]

The referee stopped the bout in the 13th round. The fight was later described as "The St. Valentine's Day Massacre." When Vikki visited Jake in his dressing room, it was a terrible scene. She described blood pouring from his nose, mouth, and face, skin shredded by Robinson's repeated blows.

Yet LaMotta, true to his spirit, repeated only one comment: "I never went down. I never went down." [9]

No, he did not hit the canvas. The price of such valor was a harsh one.

There would never be a seventh Robinson–LaMotta fight. What had once been an evenly matched rivalry was no longer.

18

Time to End It

Some might say Sugar Ray Robinson beat the hubris out of Jake LaMotta. But if so, it was a temporary condition. He did take away the middleweight championship belt, and that was the last LaMotta would see of it except in old pictures of himself.

Naturally, the first thing a defeated champion thinks about is getting the title back. Jake took such a licking that talk of a rematch against Robinson dissipated. It was not because the event wasn't popular enough—30 million watched on television. However, now everyone knew a rematch shouldn't happen. The two men's careers were headed in opposite directions.

"I didn't know it then, but that was really the end of my career," LaMotta said years later.[1]

It had been such a struggle to make weight that LaMotta did have a slight feeling of impending doom before he climbed through the ropes to face Robinson. He said he regretted betting $10,000 on himself, but knew he couldn't take that back. He asked brother Joey to give him a shot of brandy before he fought, something he had never done before.

LaMotta had not always been on friendly terms with the sportswriters covering his career and many of them savaged his effort after the Billy Fox fight. But after this difficult night, they recognized a nobility and heart in the manner in which he fought Robinson, even when he was hopelessly beaten. They turned up the praise to take note of how his last stand looked.

"Beaten to a pulp by Ray Robinson, half-blind with his title beyond hope of salvaging, Jake had one previous possession left and nothing but fierce pride to defend it with," wrote the *New York Daily Mirror*'s Dan Parker. "Jake braced himself and helplessly took everything Robinson fired at him with fortitude that made the early Spartans seem cowardly." [2]

The message Robinson delivered with his fists was that it was time for LaMotta to retire. But, LaMotta wasn't listening. He didn't want to hear any such suggestions, although he did not behave like a fighter ready to sacrifice to regain his crown. He immediately began gorging on alcohol and ill-advised meals, and his weight jumped right back up by more than 20 pounds.

Vikki said Jake was impossible to be with. Already extraordinarily jealous, she said he was delving into paranoia. The heart he showed in the ring was empty of emotion when things involved her. He also could not regain his boxing equilibrium, not training or preparing properly. LaMotta gave up on the 160-pound division as something from his past, setting his sights on moving up to light-heavyweight permanently. He was 30 years old and felt 40. He only stood 5'8" and didn't have the innate power to bang with the bigger guys. Heck, LaMotta had been no knockout artist against middleweights. Now, he had to find the strength to fend off 175-pounders. There is a difference between weighing in at a honed 175 pounds and weighing in at 175 pounds because you ate too much pasta.

Vikki said LaMotta reached the point where if they went out to dinner, he assumed she was eyeing a guy at the next table. Then, it worsened. He began stockpiling groceries all over the apartment so she did not have to go grocery shopping. In her own words, she felt like a prisoner at home.

"The situation was intolerable," Vikki said.[3]

The end was coming for Jake in the ring and in his marriage to Vikki. It was not clear which would occur first.

Jake was rude and crude in his talk with Vikki many times during the early years of their marriage, but he was not physically abusive to her, with one notable exception being in the late 1940s about a year after the marriage began. When she said something he did not like one time, Jake backhanded Vikki across the face, making her bleed, and rearranging her nose. A doctor's visit was required. Another time Vikki was foolish enough to engage in some boxing playfulness with Jake, and he hit her hard on the arm with intent.

However, after LaMotta lost to Robinson in their sixth fight and lost his title, he seemed to come unglued. Not only were his training and daily living habits bad, but Vikki said LaMotta began staying out nights partying. She saw him with another woman and was ready to leave him, but became pregnant again with their third child, so she did not.

When LaMotta returned to the ring, he began campaigning as a light-heavyweight. He realized there was no chance for him to succeed again as a middleweight. On June 27, 1951, fourth months after the Valentine's Day loss to Robinson, LaMotta met Bob Murphy at Yankee Stadium.

Actually, "Bob Murphy" was not the real name of his opponent. He was born Edwin Lee Conarty in Florida in 1922, but fought under the name "Irish Bob Murphy." He was pretty good at it, too, compiling a 65-11-2 record. LaMotta never acted with seriousness of purpose in agreeing to meet Murphy. After the Robinson fight, LaMotta's weight shot up as high as 195 pounds. He thought it would be easy to drop down to 175 pounds, but it wasn't that easy after all as almost any American dieting in a less-than-educated way could have told him.

"What I had on my side was logic and stupidity," LaMotta said of his less than clear thinking.[4]

It would have been easier on Vikki if she had followed through on her resolve to leave LaMotta when he began his decline, but she was thinking more as a mother than a wife, which was a mistake on several fronts. Much later, Vikki told a reporter that LaMotta had kept a diary when he switched from middleweight to light-heavyweight, and the parts that were quoted were pathetic for anyone, never mind someone seeking to remain a world-class boxer.

Among the words written by LaMotta in this diary were, "Alcohol seems to stay in your system and doesn't want to come out." And, "Drank too much and got sick." Also, "Ate bad, drank bad, gained eight pounds in one day."[5]

The plan against Irish Bob Murphy was for LaMotta to show off his fresh form in a new weight class, but things didn't go so well. Murphy won the fight. Murphy was a good fighter who later met Joey Maxim for the light-heavyweight belt, but lost in a 15-round decision.

On January 28, 1952, LaMotta gave it another go, this time against Norman Hayes in the Boston Garden in Massachusetts. Hayes, 24-17-1, should not have been as tough an obstacle as Murphy, but LaMotta lost a split decision to him. He had a three-fight losing streak going, and Vikki was begging him to retire. LaMotta did not view his situation as three strikes and you're out.

On March 5, 1952, LaMotta met Gene Hairston at the Olympia in Detroit, but couldn't beat him either. Hairston's lifetime mark was 43-15-5, so these guys LaMotta were facing knew their way around the ring well enough to give him trouble. LaMotta and Hairston drew.

Away from the gym and the ring, LaMotta seemed like a mess, drinking, overeating, and according to Vikki, now womanizing. Abruptly, he announced the family was going to move to Florida, a place they loved for vacations, but not as a home. She balked at first, and then realized maybe it would do Jake some good to start fresh.

To LaMotta's credit, he straightened out his boxing life sufficiently that when he signed on to meet Murphy, Hayes, and Hairston all one more time, he was able to defeat all three of them. Maybe the beach did agree with him. Perhaps the sunshine was advantageous, but by his admission in his autobiography, LaMotta attributed his rejuvenation to taking time to think (not clear about what), rest, and screw around with other women. He found that he was attractive to more women than he thought.

In later reflection, LaMotta said that his behavior then was regrettable.

"This seemed to do wonders for my mixed-up thinking about my manhood," he said of his successful babe patrol. "I came back with a new belief in myself and I devoured everything good said about me, trying to make that belief even stronger." [6]

No one was under any illusion the LaMotta of the past was back, however. He was not really making a run at the light-heavyweight crown. He was past his prime and maybe he knew it, but couldn't admit it. Also, LaMotta had no alternative career waiting in the on-deck circle that would enable him to make a living. It wasn't as if he had a college degree just waiting to be put to work for him. All he knew was fighting, and he hadn't even really thought about staying in the sport as a manager or trainer when he hung up the gloves.

Just about all LaMotta had practiced over the years was throwing punches. Worse, he was now throwing them at Vikki, too, as if his wife was just another sparring partner or six-round foe. Vikki was no longer the 16-year-old girl swept up by the glitz and glitter of being a star athlete's other half. She was more mature, had learned some things about life, and not all of her opinions were the same as Jake's. He was unable to cope with that change and if Vikki "defied" him at times, he bopped her.

Once, she asked the man she had loved and who had at least once treasured her why, after he beat her, he had done it. "He said, 'I did it because I loved you. I thought it would frighten you into coming back to me. Besides, I get hurt all the time. It doesn't mean anything.'" [7]

It sounded like the logic of a twisted, sick man.

Time and so many fights over so many years were wearing Jake down. After the heroic stand against Robinson, he never again was as sharp a fighter. He may have retained his courage, but not his skills. He kept returning to the ring thinking one day the zip would be back, and he could punch his way into becoming a light-heavyweight title contender. If he was fooling anyone, it was only himself.

On December 31, 1952, LaMotta took on another of the younger Turks he would have to get past in the division to gain a title opportunity. Danny Nardico followed LaMotta's clean-up of old debts against Hairston, Hayes, and Murphy, but he went back into debt. LaMotta lost to Nardico (again, a solid 51-13-4 lifetime) in Coral Gables, Florida.

Nardico had been a high-school football star in Ohio, a Marine in World War II and the Korean War, and won two Purple Hearts. He was definitely no pushover, and much to the surprise of LaMotta and other boxing observers, he was tough enough to become the only fighter to knock Jake down in a bout. The event occurred in the seventh round, and LaMotta was beaten by technical knockout when the referee stopped the fight.

The Ring magazine ranked Nardico fifth in the light-heavyweight class just prior to his bout against LaMotta. In theory, if LaMotta had been able to take out Nardico, he would have assumed a high slot in the ratings. Instead, Nardico accomplished something Sugar Ray Robinson could not.

That year Robinson had other things on his mind. He had defeated an aging Henry Armstrong, but he developed a goal to match Armstrong's achievement of winning championship belts in three weight classes. Armstrong had pulled off the monumental accomplishment of holding three titles at once in the original classic divisions: featherweight, lightweight, and welterweight.

Although as the weight classes expanded over time and the weight disparity between them shrunk, numerous other fighters won titles in several divisions, nobody achieved what Armstrong did. Robinson, who had won the welterweight and the middleweight titles when he beat Jake, thought big.

On June 25, 1952, although he was the opposite of LaMotta in the sense he did not gain weight easily, Robinson was granted a shot at the light-heavyweight belt held by Joey Maxim. For Robinson, moving up to the 175-class took boldness. Unlike LaMotta who could just sniff a plate of pasta and gain weight. Robinson had a hard time and weighed in at 157½ pounds, a poor fit for the division. Maxim weighed 173 points.

A tremendous heat wave hit New York and, although Robinson was piling up the points in the fight employing his usual style, he was becoming dehydrated as the suspense built at Yankee Stadium. Even the original referee, Ruby Goldstein, couldn't last the distance, and the call went out for a relief referee, Ray Miller. Goldstein and Robinson couldn't stand the heat and evacuated the kitchen, and Maxim retained his title.

Robinson collapsed from heat exhaustion at the end of the 13th round, stood up, staggered to his corner, and could not rise from his stool for the 14th round. It was said the two boxers lost 20 pounds between them during that brutal night. Goldstein and Robinson left the ring by stretcher. Many spectators in the crowd also passed out from the heat, and all they did was watch.

For LaMotta, once again the defeat to Nardico indicated messages were being sent that he ignored. This knockdown was something that hurt his pride. Never going down to the canvas meant a lot to LaMotta, but now as he was hitting athletic old age, it had happened. Later, Jake did admit, "Old stupid got his block knocked off." [8]

LaMotta did not fight again for more than a year, when he then took on Johnny Pretzie in West Palm Beach, on March 11, 1954. Pretzie was a good opponent for easing back into action. His career mark was 10-13-1, with one of those 13 losses inflicted on this occasion by Jake via technical knockout. Pretzie didn't have much luck later, either. He was shot to death in a South Boston bar in 1989.

On April 3, 1954, less than a month after topping Pretzie, LaMotta was back at work flinging leather. There was more than one fighter who competed under the name Al McCoy, but the one LaMotta beat in North Carolina was not to be confused with the Al McCoy who, decades earlier, was the middleweight world champ.

It didn't really matter what the foes' names were at this point for LaMotta, as long as he chalked up victories. Excepting the dud against Nardico, he had won five of his last six fights, which wasn't so bad. Then, just 11 days after the triumph over McCoy, LaMotta met Billy Kilgore in Miami Beach.

Kilgore was a southerner, born in Birmingham, Alabama, but living in Deland, Florida. His final record would be 39-23-4, and his greatest fame in the ring came on April 14, 1954, when his split-decision victory over former world champion Jake LaMotta ended the Bronx Bull's professional boxing career.

This loss was the last straw for Jake after 106 fights. He just knew it was time to quit. LaMotta couldn't turn back the clock or regain his skills in the ring. He was never going to be light enough to fight as a middleweight again, and he was never going to be strong enough to accomplish much as a light-heavyweight.

LaMotta had dropped out of school and had little formal education. He had earned something approaching $1 million in the ring, but had spent or squandered almost all of it. His marriage with Vikki was more than on the rocks, it was pretty much sunk, although it took time to play out the final drama.

Jake LaMotta was still shy of his 33rd birthday, and he had no idea what he wanted to do with the rest of his life. He was no deep thinker. He had no skill in the building trades. All he had done was fight for more than three decades. What else was there besides throwing punches?

19

It's Over with Vikki

By the mid-1950s, just about everything Jake LaMotta had grown up with or been identified with had passed from his life.

When he was a youngster, he was a street criminal. He had passed through that phase and gone legit. His father had thrown him into fighting as a kid, and he threw himself into boxing as a sport and livelihood as an adult. In 1954, he retired from the ring.

Vikki was LaMotta's second wife, but by 1956 after 11 years of marriage, she was sick of him and wanted out. She filed for a separation. When they divorced a year later, she made sure she got custody of the children.

LaMotta was left with one thing nobody could ever take from him. As long as he lived, and into eternity of the written word, he would forever be known as the one-time middleweight boxing champion of the world. He may have lost the belt to Sugar Ray Robinson, but he had not lost the cachet.

But LaMotta was still a young man in his early 30s, and he had to find something new to fill his time, to provide money, and to once again identify with, which did not come easy for him. LaMotta was no Renaissance man, a person of many skills and interests. His fists carried him where he needed to go as a youth and as a professional. Now, however, he had to rely on something else, something fresh.

It was a trying time for LaMotta, especially because his support system of Vikki and the children, to whatever degree they really represented support in his I'm-the-boss-and-don't-you-forget-it mind, were gone.

"Look Jake," LaMotta remembered Vikki saying, "we can't go on like this the rest of our lives. We're too young. You've got to find something to do. Something that gets you out of the house where you got something to do, and I don't want to do nothing but nag, but you'll also drink yourself to death the way you're going." [1]

LaMotta was drinking hard, admittedly propositioning anyone in a skirt, and screwing around with anyone who said yes—and according to him that was a lot of women. He didn't come home at night. He had degenerated into a shadow of the guy Vikki had once been impressed by. All the faults she attributed to Jake had pretty much always been there, but as a 16-year-old she was blind to them. As someone approaching 30 who had lived through a long decade as LaMotta's wife, she wasn't even interested in apologies, explanations, or any reasons he offered for his behavior.

LaMotta was a nightclub host in his own place, and when he went on stage, he honed an act about himself. "Let me tell you a story," it went. LaMotta had a lot of stories. Some of them were funnier than others. He had a decent sense of timing and maybe, he thought, he could make some money at this thing called "An Evening with Jake LaMotta." It wasn't Jake pummeling people to a pulp, but Jake just being Jake. LaMotta was not a first-rate comedian like others of the 1950s, no Jack Benny, Mort Sahl, or Jackie Gleason. His shtick was part vaudeville, part insult-comedy, part autobiographical. If he was a little rough around the edges, well, Jake LaMotta had always been a little rough around the edges.

He was not about to become a school teacher, a carpenter, a brick layer, or a doctor. Jake playing Jake made as much sense as anything. He happened to own his own nightclub, so he could do anything he wanted. But he was also Jake LaMotta, former middleweight champion of the world. He was a name. It was a sports name, granted, not a show business name, but Hollywood, TV studios, broadcast studios, and theatres have always been jam-packed with actor-wannabes who are refugees from the world of sports. They are not generally angling to perform Shakespeare, but merely to take the next step in life following athletic retirement.

For years, their sport was a rush for athletes, and they seemed adrift when they give up the game that made them famous. They all pass through the little death of retirement wondering what's next, what they can do to rekindle the cheers. Some are hopeless even at sports broadcasting. Some make it to the top. Others make it big in the movies.

Jim Brown may have been the greatest football player ever with the Cleveland Browns, and he was successful in Hollywood. Alex Karras was a football star before hitting it big in the flick *Blazing Saddles*. Arnold Schwarzenegger was a body builder before he became an action movie star. The Rock, Dwayne Johnson, was a college football player and professional wrestler.

In boxing, former heavyweight champ Jack Dempsey appeared in movies and even on Broadway. Another heavyweight champ, Max Baer, made his movie debut in a boxing film, *The Prizefighter and the Lady*, in 1933. Much later, heavyweight contender Randall "Tex" Cobb had a nice run as an actor in *Raising Arizona* and *The Champ*, as well as on television. It wasn't as if athletes in many sports, including boxers, had not gone the thespian route before.

Vikki was glad Jake found something to do that seemed constructive, but around the house he was as destructive as ever. He remained controlling and drank excessively. He kept wild hours, and he even came home with lipstick on his clothing not belonging to Vikki. One night she went out to dinner with friends and walked in on Jake at the bar with another woman.

"I turned and walked out," Vikki said. "He followed, caught up to me at the car, and slugged me, once, hard. The next thing I knew I was on the ground, dazed, with blood flowing from my ear and a crowd of people gathered around me. I got up in a daze."[2]

Of all things, LaMotta promptly drove her to the hospital to obtain stitches on her ear, just as if he had rescued her from a minor household accident. That was when Vikki resolved to leave him. She should have gone to the police and had LaMotta thrown in jail. In the 1950s, there was certainly a lack of support systems for battered wives, so it is impossible to theorize what would have happened if Vikki had Jake arrested. But she did not try that step.

By LaMotta's own description in *Raging Bull*, when Vikki informed him that she was obtaining a divorce, he was oblivious. He was hanging out in his nightclub "Jake's" in Miami Beach with several women and a few guys and said he had downed about a pint-and-a-half of booze. Vikki showed up and said she wanted to talk to him in private, but he wanted to introduce her to the gang. He began raving about what a terrific wife Vikki was, how she had nearly won the Mrs. America title, and how she was deserving, but he didn't want her to win because there was no way he was going to let his babe roam around alone doing all that traveling.

Vikki basically dragooned him out of earshot of those people and told him she had been to a lawyer, was getting a divorce, and had obtained a court order to keep him out of the house. LaMotta began sleeping on a cot in his office.

Eventually, Vikki left the house to Jake, took the kids, and began accepting modeling jobs to pay bills. She said she sold her furs and jewelry to raise more money, not missing them in the least. LaMotta repeatedly called her on the phone, hounding her to agree to reconciliation. She maintained the calls were conducted at high volume. He sold their house and moved into a motel a block away. When the kids were outside playing, he simply walked into Vikki's apartment, sat down, and stayed, a very unwelcome guest who pestered her about getting back together. He also continued giving her the third degree about her whereabouts on a given night and what company she kept.

From all indications, LaMotta was slowly cracking up. Vikki's description of what came next was horrifying and stomach-churning. Jake kept proclaiming his love for her and his desire to reunite the family. Until the night the former middleweight champion of the world—his claim to fame based on his fists—walked in, walked up to Vikki, and began pounding her as if the bell had just rung for round one.

Only there was no bell, no warning. He just pranced in and without saying anything began to beat her up.

"Then he slugged me," she said. "And punched me again. In the past, he'd held something back when he hit me. This time, every punch was calculated to disable and cause pain and the punches kept coming." Years later she said the mere thought of the incident made her cringe. "I still cry when I talk about it because I didn't think anyone was capable of hurting me that badly. There was nothing I could do. I was helpless and the punches kept raining down. Then fear set in. I thought Jake might actually kill me." [3]

Vikki's nose was broken and her entire chest area was left black and blue.

After that, despite seeking court orders and police protection, none of which worked, she said, Jake would just periodically show up and assault her with impunity. Vikki said she called the police, but they didn't seem to arrive in any hurry. How could they not know what was going on? The answer to her was that they did know, but apparently didn't care.

Was Jake LaMotta that big a name? Was he that big a force that he could beat the snot out of his wife as he ignored a court order and the police? There does not appear to be any rational explanation for what Vikki LaMotta endured at the hands of Jake, nor about the total lack of protection offered by the authorities.

Once Vikki ran from the house in her nightgown and a police officer did stop and ask if she was okay. Another time, meeting Jake in a restaurant, a public place, she said he put all 10 of his fingers on her forehead and raked his nails down the skin until she bled. He was nuts and out of control. He was acting the part of a sadist more than a comedian.

He couldn't beat Danny Nardico or Billy Kilgore in the ring, so he beat up Vikki LaMotta in the house. Raging Bull, was supposed to be a nickname of appreciation for Jake LaMotta. Instead, it came to more aptly describe a psychiatric disorder, it seemed. What other explanation can there be for such a compulsion? And he got away with it, every time.

For all the candor on display in Jake LaMotta's autobiography *Raging Bull*, for all the shameful acts he admitted to, there is nowhere like this level of detail about how he may have treated Vikki at his worst. Apparently, he drew a line between naked truth and full admission. Once the years had passed and Vikki died in 2006 with him outliving her by years despite being born earlier, he probably assumed no one would hear what she had to say. But 20 years after penning her life story, she revealed all the brutal secrets from their marriage. When her book, *Knockout!*, was published, she was not available to amplify, discuss, or explain it further. She laid bare her descriptions. Perhaps this was her revenge, either true to the core or exaggerated. Maybe Jake in his old age thought so, but it painted the most repellent of all possible pictures.

In the end when Jake was finally arrested, he was charged with a different kind of crime altogether. While adjudicated guilty, the entire incident actually makes it seem as if it was somewhat the result of a fabricated tale that cost him in a major way. However, it is difficult to feel too much sympathy for a man who was using his estranged wife as a punching bag. It may or may not have been backwards justice, but LaMotta certainly got his comeuppance.

LaMotta was a big name in Miami Beach. His title carried stature. He ran a popular nightclub. His own act was fledgling, but he was doing alright. He did not come off as nearly the lout in public, where people applauded him, as he did under the radar.

The way things came down as described in *Raging Bull*, both the book and movie, and in Vikki's book, was that the same cops indifferent to his pummeling Vikki nabbed Jake for another offense. LaMotta learned that if prostitution flourished in an establishment whether or not the owner was aware, he was liable. As it so happened, a girl who looked much older than her years did business at Jake's club.

In 1957, he was arrested and charged with introducing girls to men. The charge was brought by a 14-year-old girl, who could have passed for 21. She made the complaint against LaMotta. Yes, he probably did introduce her to men. The way LaMotta operated and schmoozed at his club, he probably introduced a hundred women to men. Did he knowingly promote prostitution? Likely not. There was no indication LaMotta patronized prostitutes. He claimed women threw themselves at him. Not because he was the handsomest dude in the building, but because of his fame, his boxing history, and being the main man in the club. Whatever combination of those things worked in his favor, LaMotta said he had no problems attracting women.

Jake wanted to see his patrons having fun, drinking, and living it up, and certainly he wanted the club to be known as a place where a guy could meet a girl and create sparks. It was not a bad reputation to have. That's half of the world's entertainment right there, mixing in a place, meeting new people, and hoping you find the right one.

"If that law (holding an owner liable) was really enforced, every other saloon keeper in Miami Beach would be spending his life in jail," LaMotta said in his defense. Of his club, he said, "There was good entertainment, pleasant surroundings, quiet atmosphere. I don't deny that guys could meet dolls there, just as they could anywhere else in the Beach. Single guys and single gals often came into my joint, just as they did everywhere else and if they wanted to talk to each other, what was I supposed to do, tell them to get out?" [4]

The young girl testified in court she had twice picked up men at Jake's place who paid her $20 apiece. She said she did not produce an ID indicating she was 21. Jake bent her over, kissed her, and said anyone who could kiss like that had to be 21. Big mistake. When it came to proof of age, that maneuver did not hold up as a defense in court for LaMotta.

LaMotta took the rap for aiding and abetting a prostitute and operating an establishment that encouraged that activity. He was sentenced to six months in jail, given a $500 fine, and was buried under such an avalanche of bad publicity it ruined his business. Even years later, when penning his autobiography, LaMotta said he didn't even remember the girl. He was naturally astonished when she showed up for his trial dressed more like a 14-year-old than a hooker on the prowl.

That was the end of LaMotta as a club owner in Miami Beach. His life was in shambles. Vikki got her divorce. He had driven away the woman he loved the most. He had driven away his children. He had lost the business that represented his future. LaMotta went to jail.

In a dramatic and famous scene in the movie *Raging Bull*, actor Robert De Niro as Jake goes wild with frustration as he is led to his cell. It is obvious Jake is boiling over, at a loss to understand what he has done to deserve this incarceration. In the film, he bangs his head against the wall in his cell and in rapid fire motion punches the wall with both fists. It is an unyielding concrete wall, a substance that will not give way to his punches. By repeatedly hitting the wall, he can only harm himself further. As he had done so many times during his life, that is exactly what the real Jake LaMotta did.

It took him way too long to figure that all out. Long into retirement he told a sportswriter, "The truth of the matter? The punches never hurt me. My nose was broken six times, my hands six times, a few fractured ribs. Fifty stitches over my eyes. But the only place I got hurt was out of the ring." [5]

20

The Marrying Kind

At the peak of his self-destructive partying days, Jake LaMotta bedded any woman who threw herself at him. He drank long and hard and took no care of his once-athletic body.

Married once before he met Vikki, his second wife and arguably his real true love (even obsession), LaMotta had finally lost his Svengali grip on her. They separated and then divorced.

But when it came to marriage, LaMotta was never shy. He didn't just date, he visited the altar. LaMotta ended up with more wives than he did bouts against Sugar Ray Robinson. Ladies whose last names changed to LaMotta outnumbered fights versus Sugar Ray seven to six.

LaMotta was a serial marrying man, seemingly almost a husband for hire. He did fall in love a lot. Over the course of his life, LaMotta was married for many years, just not to one woman. His anniversaries never approached the gold or silver level of gift-giving.

In Jake's case, it was that you couldn't tell his wife of the moment without a scorecard. It all became particularly confusing when periodically he once again tried to inject himself into Vikki's life.

Keeping up with Jake's marriages was exhausting. You had to be a famous gossip columnist like Earl Wilson or Walter Winchell to get the names straight. Anyone else needed a cheat sheet. It wasn't as if LaMotta seemed to learn anything from his harrowing experiences with Vikki either, like how to treat a lady, how to cherish a wife, or how to make a relationship last.

LaMotta met his third wife when he was still in Miami, when things were going down the drain with Vikki. Jake fell for Sally, and he praised her for standing by her man while he did his time in jail. A model, she was celebrating her 19th birthday at a hotel when he first spied her and made a move.

Who knows what LaMotta really told her about his personal history, though he admitted getting too drunk, and talking about his legal problems and his Vikki woes. Ordinarily, such subjects would not be winning conversation strategies, but Sally was a good listener and seemed taken by him.

"She was a good kid, a real sweetheart," LaMotta said. "Everything that Vikki wasn't. . . Sally would bring my kids to the jail to visit me. She really stuck by me when the rest of them acted like LaMotta was some kind of new social disease. Yeah, Sally was a real good sport." [1]

Just what kind of show LaMotta put on when he was wooing Sally is not clear, but most people are at their best in the courtship stages before day-to-day reality sets in. Marriage is for the long run and it all eventually comes out. In LaMotta's case, he had a few bad habits that could be lousy for the health of a weaker female partner, as Vikki learned.

Strangely, when Sally was several years younger and living in an orphanage, she saw Jake on TV with Rocky Graziano on "The Martha Raye Show." She liked the way he looked and came off. Sally never even expected to meet LaMotta, but the next thing she knew she was dating him, and he was proposing marriage to her.

Sally was quite naïve—Jake even referred to her as his baby, probably thinking this was another young, good-looking woman he could control. By the time they got around to talking marriage, Sally was 22, and Jake was 37. Her only ideal of a man stemmed from a grandfather who was tough and stern, and LaMotta kind of reminded her of him.

LaMotta had air-lifted Sally out of Miami to New York where she didn't know anyone. He made her dependent on him, much the way Vikki had been as a teenager. It was not as if all their time spent together was idyllic. Jake was still Jake, with the same characteristics.

Whether it was the typical bridal nerves, or a little voice inside her head announcing that maybe marrying Jake was not the best idea, Sally's wedding day mental outlook seemed to resemble Vikki's. There was a heavy dose of "What am I doing?" in her thoughts.

On their wedding night, Jake and Sally visited the Copacabana night club. Comedian Joe E. Lewis was performing, and he recognized LaMotta in the audience. He introduced him as the former boxing champ and when the crowd cheered for him Lewis called him up on stage.

When Lewis asked him what was new, LaMotta said, "And all of you beautiful girls out there are gonna be sad, but I gotta tell ya I just got married today to a beautiful, gorgeous, sexy, young princess named Sally." What began innocently rapidly descended into ugliness. A heckler asked him why he was twice-divorced and LaMotta bristled when the guy shouted, "She get tired of bein' your punchin' bag, you phony bum?" [2]

LaMotta almost plunged into the crowd to attack the irritant. Lewis tried to calm him down, and the audience became uncomfortable.

"You know, it's guys like you that are gonna force me to make a comeback," LaMotta said.[3]

That was actually a pretty snappy retort.

Still, LaMotta came quite close to blowing his cool with more than words. As he left the stage, he did have a verbal tête-á-tête with Walter Winchell, who made the error of saying Vikki sent her regards. LaMotta nearly attacked him. Mind you, this was supposed to be a happy occasion, not a terribly auspicious one for Sally as it turned out.

Jake had not foregone drinking. He came home sloshed, barely able to stand, threw up in his and Sally's apartment, and at one point she accused him of being drunk for two of the first three months they were married. Jake's princess was not having tons of fun. They had a loud-decibel confrontation after LaMotta came home plowed after being left off the guest list for a Sugar Ray Robinson shindig. Sally informed him she had flushed his Scotch and tore into him.

"I wouldn't invite you anywhere," she said. "Just look at yourself. You're turning into a champion slob."[4]

It was difficult to win a war of words with Jake, not because his vocabulary was so slick, but because if he didn't like what he heard he might flip out and take it out physically on his antagonist. It did not matter if the person was his wife, or was weaker and smaller.

On this occasion, LaMotta attacked Sally, not with his fists, but by wrapping his hands around her neck and nearly squeezing the life out of her. He only stopped choking her when he keeled over unconscious, presumably because he was so drunk. Sally claimed LaMotta was so out of it he thought she was Vikki and intended to kill Vikki.

Sally intended seeking a divorce right then, but the next day was informed she was pregnant, so she stuck around a little while longer. A baby girl was added to the family. Of course, that only temporarily staved off a split. Jake wasn't going to change, and Sally wasn't going to find any happiness with a carousing drunken husband who was subject to violent outbursts.

Just as he had done as a boxer, LaMotta left a trail of crumpled and demoralized bodies in his wake, this time amongst those who loved him the most.

"When a broad like Sally makes up her mind, it's over for good," LaMotta said. "I learned that the hard way. Every time she and the kids moved, I'd find them and every time there'd be an ugly scene. She got a Mexican divorce on our anniversary." [5]

LaMotta didn't seem to take any responsibility as the possible instigator of those scenes.

When LaMotta met his fourth wife, Petra, one of his first comments to her upon informing her that he was not married was, "Right now I'm not married. I'm tryin' to cool it for a while. But ya gotta keep tryin' until ya get it right, I guess." [6]

It wasn't clear if LaMotta was trying to impress Petra or test her, but his autobiography, *Raging Bull*, had just come out, and he gave her an autographed copy. It was pretty much Jake unvarnished, if not 100 percent complete, but it wasn't the same as sending a fresh face some flowers. There was a lot of negative Jake in the volume, so maybe he figured if he didn't scare her away with his words, he might have a chance.

Petra was honest enough with LaMotta to tell him the truth when he asked if she just liked him or was attracted to him being a fighter—being a boxer did factor into her thinking. Whatever it was, it didn't take long before Petra became Mrs. LaMotta Number Four.

His book was so new that he took Petra on the promotional book tour. LaMotta was totally smitten with Petra's beauty, but they had gotten married quickly, and he only began to really know her after they were hitched. He wasn't always happy with what he got. LaMotta said Petra had many phobias. She feared flying. He also noted she worked to attract attention. Jake was supposed to be the number-one attraction on tour. He had demonstrated tremendous levels of jealousy when one of his wives was looked at, appreciated, talked to, or even just conducted a civil conversation.

If you traveled with Jake, you ranked second to him. He was the one who was supposed to light up a room and have all the attention focused on him. He talked about wanting to show off Petra, or his beautiful wives, but pretty much couldn't stand it when anyone noticed them.

One day on tour, Petra did not join Jake for an early-morning television interview, saying she was suffering from a migraine. His reaction?

"Broads, every time you count on them for something, they come up with some stupid excuse," LaMotta said. "If it's not a headache, then they got their period, or a run in their stockings or something." He was bucking for misogynist of the year apparently. "Broads. . . just because they've got a slit between their legs, they think they have it made. All they think they gotta do is lay there and some jerk will kiss their ass and pay all their bills. Vikki was the same way—I couldn't trust her as far as I could throw her." [7]

That was the usual coarse Jake, rude and crude, even when discussing his wives, perhaps especially when discussing his wives. After Petra went shopping instead of attending a meeting where LaMotta wanted to make a good impression, he returned to his hotel room and spanked her bare bottom. It was his method of punishing her for not listening to what he said, and he made the point of noting that you couldn't just belt a dame these days because if she showed up in public with a black eye, the newspapers would get wind of it. That's why a spanking worked better.

It was Petra who spoke up for a divorce, but this time LaMotta did not beg or try to convince his wife to stay. Thinking more clearly than normally, he thought it might be a good idea to split up with this wife.

There would be more wives, of course. LaMotta met his next wife in an elevator. Her name was Debbie, and she became number five on the hit parade. At the time, he was working as a bouncer at a New York club, but that job ended after he punched out a customer. The matter was resolved without legal charges filed, but also with his exit from the position.

He did promptly ingratiate himself enough with Debbie after the off-beat meeting while descending from a high floor of a building to the lobby. He kept after her for a date, calling her repeatedly until she yielded. Then, a date became another date, and things went from there until the marrying man had a new wife.

Essentially, Jake wore Debbie down. She resisted his entreaties until finally meeting him for a drink. When she first saw his apartment, she was appalled. This wasn't the best time in Jake's life. He had lost his club, been divorced a couple of times, wasn't working steadily at a job that produced much income, and his place was shabby with little of note in it and empty walls. It was a pretty depressing environment. More credit to LaMotta for building on such a shaky beginning to get this woman to fall in love with him.

It wasn't as if Debbie's seconds in her corner were backing this relationship either. She had a sister who was negative about Jake and a mother who didn't even want her to go out on the first date.

When they married Jake and Debbie were wed in a small, private ceremony. When he slipped the ring on her finger he said, "This'll never end, Debbie darling." [8] No Nostradamus, that Jake.

For a time, LaMotta's ability to make a living just being Jake had run its course. He took a liquor salesman's job. Certainly, he knew the product. Put a few drinks in LaMotta and it was always possible he would make a scene, get angry, insult someone, or slug his wife. It was a trap that he couldn't escape—the worst of his character was brought out when fueled by booze.

At one point in the 21 Club in New York, LaMotta was pumping down too many brandies for the bartender's taste, and he warned Jake he might have to cut him off. Almost immediately, LaMotta threatened to beat him up. Debbie was embarrassed and disgusted, telling him he was pissing off too many people because he was busy sounding like Al Capone. LaMotta's defense was that none of the guys he made such threats to took him seriously because he was only funning. Debbie informed him that yes, they did take him seriously. Of course, LaMotta reacted as expected, insulting her, calling her a dumb broad.

LaMotta lost the sales job, kept drinking, fell into a depression, and predictably tension mounted between him and Debbie. However, the opportunity to make a movie out of LaMotta's life story arose when they were together and in financial straits. In LaMotta's mind, the money would rescue the marriage.

Things did not actually play out that way. When work began on the film *Raging Bull*, Vikki came back into the picture because she was the main female character. She and Debbie apparently stared darts at one another with Jake either oblivious to it all or indifferent. He seemed to once again drift towards his old flame, Vikki, and Debbie felt humiliated. Debbie and Vikki argued, and Jake seemed to take Vikki's side.

LaMotta's strong points were neither tact nor sensitivity, so it was no surprise he was no diplomat at mediating a situation that he was in the middle of with two wives. A man in that circumstance should come through for his current wife, not his ex, but it almost seemed as if LaMotta was railroading Debbie towards an unhappy finish.

When Debbie decided to split, she found an opportunity none of the other wives were afforded. LaMotta was in the chips with a $40,000 advance check for the flick. In a cute way, Debbie kind of robbed a bank. She went to their bank carrying the check and asked to have it cashed. The LaMottas had a joint account, and the bank came through. She walked out of the bank carrying a large bag brimming with cash. Debbie considered that to be her alimony payment just in case nothing else was forthcoming. Having watched LaMotta operate, throwing money around even when he could not afford it, or spending it on drinking and partying, she had every reason to believe she would otherwise never see any money from him.[9]

It was a pretty solid scheme, especially when the bank offered no resistance. LaMotta was astonished and angry when he first deciphered what happened. But he also confidently predicted Debbie would get to thinking, get scared, and come back toting the loot.

LaMotta knew his woman. Debbie swiftly returned carrying the bag with all the money. She cried and he forgave her. As the late 1970s turned to 1980, they were back together. However, things were not all hunky-dory. Feeling stressed almost all the time, Debbie took up gambling and became addicted to the action. She oversaw weekly poker games at their home, taking the house cut. They had a scene at P. J. Clarke's, the famous New York watering hole where LaMotta had become a regular.

Once, Debbie called the cops on Jake before he actually did anything, just on general principles. They made him spend the night somewhere else. The relationship devolved into more arguments. Debbie also began drinking heavily. They gambled together at cards, and once in a dispute, Debbie threw a glass of wine in LaMotta's face before she passed out cold on the floor. Clearly, the marriage was doomed and wife number five was in the record books.

LaMotta could have just dated for the rest of his life. He could have drifted into a permanent arrangement with a partner, but he never gave up seeking wedded bliss. Wife number six was Theresa. Sugar Ray Robinson was best man for that LaMotta wedding. They didn't hit each other during that event.

Jake and Theresa met in a bar in Las Vegas while LaMotta was posing for photographers with Rocky Graziano. The best part was that even though Theresa recognized Graziano, she had no idea who the other guy was. Jake was stunned to hear that when he moseyed over and declared they had to have a drink together.

He arranged to meet her later because he had business to attend to, and Theresa had pretty much given up on him showing when he appeared at 2:45 a.m. Vegas never sleeps, and Jake wasn't indulging in much of it either. He dragged her into the casino and promptly lost all $2,500 he had just been paid. Nice first impression, huh?

They began an affair. Eventually Theresa moved to New York and gave marriage with Jake a shot. Maybe she hadn't read *Raging Bull* or seen the movie. When she was moved to Manhattan, LaMotta didn't even remember to pick her up at the airport, didn't even remember inviting her to move in with him, and then showed off his dingy studio apartment, which immediately turned her off. Day one screamed, "Big mistake."

Meanwhile, Vikki had started a makeup company, and Jake suggested she give Theresa a job. That was clear thinking. For Theresa, there didn't even seem to be a honeymoon period with LaMotta. She was shocked when he began hitting her. One Christmas, she took violently ill and began vomiting, including vomiting up blood. For some reason, as she pleaded to be taken to the hospital, LaMotta called Vikki and asked what to do. True or not, Vikki was later quoted as manipulating Jake with a comment that Theresa was probably faking it because she had told Vikki long before she was going to leave Jake on that night.[10]

It's difficult to know just what to believe in such scenarios, but life around LaMotta was such a soap opera that even an anecdote, as awfully as it would reflect on Vikki, can't be dismissed out of hand. This was a triangle of people who did not like one another.

LaMotta took Theresa to the emergency room at Lenox Hill Hospital via taxi cab. The diagnosis was a bleeding ulcer. When Theresa returned home, Jake was nice to her, stopped drinking for a while, and took care of her. He had feared for her life.

Eventually another blow-up followed. If Jake is to be believed, it was started by Vikki squealing on Theresa, telling him Theresa had screwed around with another guy. Driven to distraction by LaMotta's jealousy, Theresa left him.

Years passed and LaMotta, who never would have foreseen true old age for himself, passed through his 70s, 80s, and into his 90s. In December 2012, LaMotta announced he was going to get married for the seventh time. His new bride was Denise Baker, then 62. After meeting in 1992, they became companions after they had done some show business work together. The marriage was set for January

4, 2013, in Arizona. When the news leaked out, Baker was asked if the newlyweds were going to embark on a honeymoon.

"At Jake's age, we'll have to come home and take a nap," she said. Later, Baker would refer to LaMotta in interviews as being sweet, kind, and sensitive. Other former wives never said such things publicly.

The first to write of LaMotta's impending nuptials was the *New York Post*'s Page Six gossip section. The former champ, who likely didn't know the answer to the question, was asked where all six of the previous Mrs. LaMottas were.

"I think all of them were eaten," he said.[11]

In 2015, after years of almost being in the works, a follow-up movie to LaMotta's *Raging Bull* story was shown. It was called *The Bronx Bull*, partially to differentiate it from star director Martin Scorsese's work.

The book, *Raging Bull II, Continuing the Story of Jake LaMotta*, spends much more time providing details about LaMotta's other marriages that came after Vikki. When the movie made its debut in California, LaMotta showed up to usher it into celluloid history at the Newport Beach Film Festival.

In April 2015, LaMotta hadn't seen the final cut. It turned out to be no *Raging Bull*, but it was not for lack of trying. Several well-known actors had parts, including William Forsythe as Jake, Tom Sizemore, Joe Mantegna, Paul Sorvino, Cloris Leachman, and Penelope Ann Miller.

"I'm looking forward to seeing it," he said. "Everybody in that movie does a great job. The picture turned out to be a beautiful picture. And God bless everybody in the picture." [12]

LaMotta said the story picked up where *Raging Bull* left off, and it also told a more complete version of his childhood. He was confident it was accurate. Given so much reckless living, it was a wonder to many that LaMotta had reached 92 years of age. It sounded as if he was one of those people.

"I had such a crazy life," he said. "How I got away with it I don't know. I should have been dead a long time ago." [13]

LaMotta still traveled and Baker accompanied him on his public appearances. Being the seventh Mrs. LaMotta and not latching onto Jake until he was so old pretty much assured that, if nothing, else she was going to be the last wife.

21

Billy Fox Haunts

Jake LaMotta betrayed himself when he agreed to take a dive against Billy Fox at the behest of the mob in 1947, and it forever haunted him. He had wanted to go all the way on his own, and he was robbed of that when he was instructed to lose on purpose if he ever wanted to get a shot at the middleweight title.

LaMotta despised the circumstances he was forced into, hated the crooks tainting his sport, and through all the ups and downs of his status, sought to retain one principle of honesty by avoiding the bad guys.

Yet, he could not do so. LaMotta finally yielded to the pressure and threw his bout against Fox on November 14, 1947, at Madison Square Garden. LaMotta reluctantly committed the crime, but rather than make a clean getaway, he did such a terrible job of acting that everyone immediately suspected the result was faked.

The incident always ate at LaMotta's innards. There was a taint to his career that he could not completely shake despite all the true labor, sweat, and blood he poured into it. The fake fight would have stayed a secret amongst a small corps of people if not for two things.

For starters, if LaMotta had been able to provide a more elaborate sales job in the ring, few people would have ever connected him with a fix. Secondly, years later after he retired, the federal government undertook an investigation of the inner workings of professional boxing.

The LaMotta–Fox fight did not stay buried once scrutiny began. The stink at the time that resulted in LaMotta's suspension and fine still resonated for researchers when they went back in time to explore how organized crime had sunk its teeth into the sport. In 1960, that's how LaMotta found himself holding a subpoena to testify before a U.S. Senate committee in Washington, D.C.

This shed new public light on the shameful episode that marked LaMotta's career. Since LaMotta was retired, it was not going to harm him in terms of ring opportunity. But, it would expose the shady dealings surrounding the Fox bout and do damage to Jake's reputation. While LaMotta hated being forced into singing, a part of him was relieved that the dark side of the sport would be examined and perhaps fixed.

The Senate Subcommittee on Anti-Trust and Monopoly convened under Tennessee Senator Estes Kefauver in mid-June. The investigation focused on crime figures Blinky Palermo and Frankie Carbo, both of whom were well-known to LaMotta for their influence in the fight game.

When the government reached out to LaMotta, he dreaded the moment he had to appear before the committee. The very beginning of the book *Raging Bull II* focuses on Jake's last steps into the Senate Office Building—the condemned man's walk into the fire 13 years after the fix.

"I never did like Washington," he said. "All those oversized buildings and monuments made me feel like some dumb bug crawling around a pyramid or something. I guess I was about as alone as any one guy could get. The middleweight champion of the world was about to admit to the greatest sin in boxing. What a shit feeling—like going to confession for the first time. I was in a cold sweat." [1]

LaMotta was nervous because he intended to tell the truth about what happened, and he knew the repercussions would be embarrassing and perhaps even stronger. Joey LaMotta was called to testify, too, and he took the

Fifth Amendment more than 50 times. Carbo, who was in prison, was brought in to testify, and he also took the Fifth Amendment more than 50 times. Jake came in without a lawyer and bared his soul.

"I didn't mind admitting to my part in the deal," LaMotta said. "I wanted to come clean. I wasn't exactly proud of it, but I did what I had to in order to get my rightful shot at the title. The statute of limitations was up on the whole goddamn mess by now anyway." [2]

Jake knew that Joey was going to plead the Fifth Amendment, and he decided to accept all the blame for what happened so Joey the middle man would not be thrown under the bus. In testimony under oath, Jake said, "after a couple of weeks I received an offer of $100,000 to lose to Billy Fox, which I refused. I said I was only interested in the championship fight. It was said it could be arranged, a championship fight might be arranged. (More discussions followed). But toward the end, when I realized I couldn't possibly win, I said I would lose to Billy Fox if I was guaranteed a championship fight." [3]

LaMotta laid out the whole sordid business, with one tricky twist. He pinned his knowledge of the bribe offer solely on Joey, knowing he was going to take the Fifth Amendment, and he did not want to directly name any mobsters. Joey had been the messenger. In saying this, Jake did alter prior testimony from the New York investigation, but if his story was to be believed, he had not met with the mobsters and directly been given an ultimatum. Jake came clean, but he didn't feel clean. He was still bothered by having to fix a fight to obtain what he knew he deserved—an opportunity to fight for the crown.

"I felt like I'd been back in the ring with Ray Robinson pounding me up against the ropes for 13 rounds 'til referee

Frank Sikora jumped between us and stopped the fight," LaMotta said.[4]

Attention did not cease the moment LaMotta walked out of the hearing room. Reaction was swift and furious back in New York and in newspapers trumpeting Jake's admission about the fixed fight. Until then, there had been many suspicions about fraudulent fights, but no admission by anyone involved in a bum deal. Whether LaMotta ever thought about the response to his words before he uttered them or was just being naïve, he said he never expected the firestorm of publicity.

Some newspapers revisited the reportage on the fight to lay out for readers how the bout was perceived when it took place. LaMotta was still a fairly young man, not yet 40 years old, when his appearance in Washington was dissected. He still had a long time to live with his mistake.

"I regretted it the rest of my life," he said. "But it happened, and I had a good reason for it. All I wanted to do was become a champion. I wanted a shot at the title, and I finally did after I did what I did. I think I was wrong. It could have ruined my whole life."[5]

LaMotta's life and career were like switchback highways, with twists and turns that seemed to come out of the blue. His lowest ebb was probably when he threw the fight to Fox. Another low point was when he shed light on the corrupt deal in 1960. He tormented himself almost relentlessly over his performance against Fox, which was maybe the worst punishment he could have received.

Anyone who knows boxing history remembers the LaMotta–Fox fix. Jake is tarred by the label of being someone who once did the unthinkable—losing on purpose. Yet somehow, too, he has managed to avoid having the incident completely overrun his life. There are Hall of Fame—-caliber baseball players whose deeds were so superior on the field they rank highly on Major League Baseball's all-time lists. But the suspicion of their taking performance-enhancing drugs, much of it not formally proven, has kept them from being elected to the Hall.

What is worse in the pantheon of sport no-no's, LaMotta deliberately losing a fight or Pete Rose betting on baseball? LaMotta bears the burden of the Fox debacle, but he has in some ways transcended it. He is enshrined in the International Boxing Hall of Fame, which is a forgiveness of sorts. Ask Rose, banned for life from baseball and from his name even appearing on a Hall of Fame ballot, if he would trade situations with LaMotta.

LaMotta had to live with his crime for 70 years, but everywhere he went, he was introduced as the former middleweight champion of the world, not as a pariah for his indiscretion. Most of the time, the Fox matter did not come up. When he wrote *Raging Bull*, published in 1970, he told the truth about what happened. In 1980, when the *Raging Bull* movie came out, it dealt with the Fox fight in an unflinching manner.

It would have been interesting (with 20-20 hindsight) if movie goers had been polled on their opinions about the Fox fight portrayal. Once, Jake said he gave some women copies of his biography so they could learn about him, but they told him that they did not believe all it contained. They thought there must have been embellishments in the most extreme stories. Using that as a backdrop, it can be wondered if some film attendees thought the Fox plot twist was a Hollywood invention or exaggeration. Maybe they believed it was a blend of fact and fiction instead of an accurate depiction of LaMotta's life.

LaMotta could never outrun his past, but in a peculiar way he outlived it. Many later forums of his post-boxing life were a series of true confessions, whether in books or movies. No one has said more bad stuff about Jake LaMotta than Jake LaMotta. The Encyclopedia of Jake brims with harsh anecdotes.

Reading about Jake in his own words, one learns about his childhood crimes, his near-murder of Harry Gordon, spending time in prison, throwing a fight, poor treatment of his early wives, a long orgy of bacchanalia, drunken episodes, blowing through money, and poor business decisions. Even if he did not include everything, it is difficult to picture anyone being much harder on LaMotta than LaMotta. Though some of his wives, who suffered the worst of Jake, gave it a good run.

If LaMotta had sought work in the boxing field, as a manager, trainer, or promoter, the blight of the Fox fight would have lingered in the public eye longer and would have interfered with his ability to make a living. He would not have been welcomed so readily into those jobs after his admission.

There is little indication LaMotta gave a thought to those aspects of the boxing business after he stopped fighting. When the poorly educated LaMotta hung up his gloves and was groping in the dark for a rest-of-his-life plan, the idea list did not include those working behind the scenes in the sport. For LaMotta, life had been a survival sport from the time he was very young. He had always depended on himself and always come through.

However, he was not going back to high school, not going to enroll in college, and not going to become a doctor, lawyer, or engineer. When in doubt, just be Jake. For most of the six-and-a-half decades that followed the end of his reign as middleweight champ, LaMotta engaged in stage or film work.

When he owned his own nightclub, Jake could put himself on as a featured act. He worked other nightclubs with middling success as a stand-up comic telling personal sto-ries. Sometimes he gave solo dramatic readings. There was never an indication that LaMotta was unable to obtain a gig because he threw a fight to Billy Fox. He rose or fell on his performance.

Inspired to act by fellow champ Rocky Graziano, even-tually LaMotta did get real parts in pictures. He was a waiter in *The Hustler* with Paul Newman. LaMotta also ap-peared in such movies as *Mob War*, *Hangmen*, *Firepower*, and *Confessions of a Psycho Cat*. Unlike *The Hustler*, these were not Oscar-worthy productions.

A few years after LaMotta testified in D.C., he was es-sentially a full-time actor. His notoriety was not such that it prevented him from getting jobs. His name was well-known, but his face not so much. In the mid-1960s, LaMotta played Big Julie well off Broadway in a stage production of *Guys and Dolls*. Co-stars were Hugh O'Brian and Anita Bryant. He stuck with that role through productions in dif-ferent cities and did make it to New York for a while. The irony of LaMotta playing a hood after all his tribulations with organized crime was seemingly overlooked.

It turned out, wrapped around his domestic difficulties and high-profile discomfort with the U.S. Senate, LaMotta had spent time taking drama lessons in New York. Acting became a second calling for him.

"I was bitten by the bug," he said. "I love it. It sure beats boxing. You don't get all cut and hurt." [6]

In his joking stage appearances, LaMotta often ridiculed his marriages. In the case of his first wife, he gave a reason why they split up. "She divorced me because I clashed with the drapes," he said. [7]

He also made fun of himself.

"There's too much violence in the world," LaMotta said. "Most of it perpetrated on me by Sugar Ray Robinson." And he joked about old pal Rocky Graziano, too, imitating his manager asking Rocky, "How would you like to fight for the crown?" with Rocky responding, "Uh, I can take Queen Elizabeth in three." [8]

LaMotta also did not consider it much of a stretch for a boxer to become an actor anyway.

"Us prize fighters," he said, "appear in front of thousands of people with hardly any clothes on. We're proud. We're not ashamed of our builds. We know we got the stuff. We're all exhibitionists. We love the audience and the feeling of being a celebrity." [9]

LaMotta also performed *An Evening with Jake LaMotta* in New York. Although it has been said boxers take so much punishment from hits to the head that they lose their memories, LaMotta memorized 10,000 words for delivery to his audience, quoting from nine plays.

In one interview, LaMotta was asked about his acting limitations, and he proudly announced he had none and that if given the opportunity he would not shy away from singing and dancing, doing ballet, and performing Shakespeare.

Sometimes audience hecklers gave LaMotta bad reviews with snide comments, but professional critics seeing him in movies and plays, were kinder than not. The ultimate irony of all this went beyond playing Big Julie. Boxing is realism times 10, but the one time LaMotta was supposed to act a part in the ring he failed. He just couldn't play the role of a fighter losing on purpose on that stage with Billy Fox.

The lousy performance cost him his dignity, colored his reputation, and labeled him. As LaMotta said, the choice to throw the fight to Fox could have destroyed his life. It affected it, derailed it some ways, yet he pushed beyond it.

Once, reflecting on the Fox matter, LaMotta was as philosophical as he ever got.

"He was no fighter," Jake said. "I could have knocked him out in one round. I was the uncrowned champ for five years, but nobody wanted to fight me. I was getting older by then and I felt time was running out. And I figured the only way to get a chance to fight for the title was to do what I had to do. But, to tell you the truth, if I had to go it all over again, I'd do the same thing." [10]

22

Going Hollywood

The book *Raging Bull* had been out for a while before the team of director Martin Scorsese and actor Robert De Niro became fascinated by Jake LaMotta's story and turned it into an epic film. The movie was made about the latter part of Jake's life.

By the late 1970s, LaMotta was well into his fifties. His was a name linked to the past. For all his fame achieved in the 1940s and 1950s, the average boxing fan knew little about him beyond his name or that he once owned the middleweight crown. As far as mainstream America went, he was not at all remembered.

Instead, the making of *Raging Bull* reminded the world who he had been, who he was, and that he was still around, even if it was far from a flattering portrayal. That's what happens when you write a dramatic tale bursting with lurid truth and then trust someone else to transform that truth to the screen. The most incredible achievement of Scorsese and De Niro was bringing LaMotta alive so perfectly.

The movie was nominated for eight Academy Awards. De Niro won best actor in a grand on-screen performance that echoed his legendary preparation. More than 35 years after the movie made its debut, it is still favorably and positively reviewed, and, more than anything else, responsible for LaMotta remaining in the public eye.

The book was written by LaMotta with friend Peter Savage and Joe Carter, and it was copyrighted in 1970. Savage worked harder than anyone to get it into print, to promote it, and then sell it to the movies. That was a long struggle and LaMotta was in needy straits when the big call came through culminating in the movie deal. Two years had passed since De Niro expressed interest.

Various scripts were tried and rejected, and Vikki became a more and more important character in the rewriting. She was Jake's wife during the most important part of his boxing career, and there was no way around that. Of course, Jake and Vikki were not even speaking by the time the movie making rolled around, so that was an obstacle. Given what she put up with from Jake, she wanted no part of being portrayed in a movie without a say in how she came off. Jake received a $78,000 advance, which he sorely needed. Vikki wanted in.

When LaMotta met Debbie he gave her an autographed copy of *Raging Bull*. He told her she wouldn't like him if she read it. When she did, she thought it was mostly fiction rather than a true story.[1] When the movie was being filmed, portraying Jake in a less-than-flattering light, Debbie protested to him saying she thought he said most of the stuff was made up. LaMotta squirmed and rather than outright admitting his falsehood to her and told De Niro "If it's good for the movie, use it."[2]

"This is really gonna be big-time," LaMotta told Debbie. "I'm gonna buy ya a fur coat—maybe two—and no more cryin' about the rent. I'm gonna pay it up six months in advance. It's like bein' champ all over again."[3]

Things started rolling in 1977. De Niro was 34 and a native New Yorker from Greenwich Village. Three years earlier, he had won the Oscar for best supporting actor for his performance in *The Godfather Part II*. He had already appeared in *Bang the Drum Slowly, Mean Streets, Taxi Driver,* and *New York, New York*. He was a hot property in Hollywood, a guy who took on meaty, serious roles.

Nothing before or since, however, could match his portrayal of Jake LaMotta when it came to meaty and serious. Rarely has any actor so thoroughly and devotedly immersed himself in a role. De Niro became LaMotta. He did not merely sign up for boxing lessons, but he boxed hundreds of rounds as LaMotta tutored him in his style. De Niro studied and researched, and that was before filming even began. Later, filming was halted for a time as De Niro ate himself into a 60-pound weight gain to turn himself into a retired, aging LaMotta.

De Niro was working on the movie *1900* in Italy when he read *Raging Bull* and told Scorsese to read it. De Niro said the book had heart and potential as a film. He said that when he was a kid in New York, he sometimes saw LaMotta working in front of clubs as a bouncer and was surprised he had gotten so fat.

In Vikki's mind, there were fabrications in *Raging Bull*, and she didn't like that. If anything, she said it made Jake out to be worse than he was, and he was bad enough already. She indicated initially Jake had worked behind her back to get a release saying she would cooperate fully so he could get the advance money. She said when she found out some of the things that were going on, she very much wanted to be involved in the production so the truth would out. Vikki said there was considerable angst having to cope with Jake again in person and in reliving parts of her life that were in the past. Twenty years had passed since Vikki was with Jake, and it all mentally came rushing back. Plus, it was aggravating all over again fighting with him over what the movie should include.

"Jake still didn't understand the difference between right and wrong," she said. "He'd gotten older without getting wiser." [4]

Both Jake and Vikki, in different ways, were tremendously impressed by De Niro. Vikki said Bobby (that's what he told Jake and Vikki to call him, not Robert) had perfectly captured LaMotta's way of speaking after his nose had been busted up and his voice became more nasally. Jake was so proud of De Niro's boxing ability after the extended workouts and training that he believed he could have turned pro and held his own in real fights.

"De Niro is probably one of the greatest actors who ever lived," LaMotta said. "I can't believe anybody else would have put the time and effort that he put into that movie. Before we shot one foot of film we actually trained for about a year in the ring—over 1,000 rounds. Can you believe that?

"I showed him how to throw different punches, how to throw a left hook, how to throw a right hook, how to block punches and things like that. I also showed him films of some of my fights. When I got done teaching De Niro after a solid year I felt positive he could have fought professional. That's how dedicated he was. I don't know exactly how far he would have gone, but he would have been a pretty good professional fighter." [5]

De Niro remembered well those sessions when interviewed about the film on his 70th birthday.

"I sparred with people with gear on, but we were careful," De Niro said. "We weren't looking to kill anyone. Then I trained with Jake. He would say, 'Hit me, don't worry, don't worry.' He was 55, but he was really tough. I didn't realize until I got to his age that you could still take a punch." [6]

The filmmakers cast a young unknown to play Vikki. Vikki was 15 when she met Jake and 16 when they married. Cathy Moriarty, from the Bronx, was 19 when she played Vikki. They met and Vikki liked her. In her first role, Moriarty earned a best supporting actress nomination for *Raging Bull* and was nominated for four more acting awards for playing Vikki.

Like Moriarty, the actor cast to play Joey, Jake's brother, was unknown at the time. It was Joe Pesci. At the time, Pesci had had one bit part and one significant performance in another film. He was nominated for an Academy Award for best supporting actor in *Raging Bull* and later won that award for the movie *Goodfellas*.

LaMotta said De Niro wanted everything to be authentic. One of the things about *Raging Bull* that made it look authentic was Scorsese's decision to film in black and white. It was a gritty movie with a gritty feel. Initially, it was seen as too grim and too violent by many, which slowed its popular reception.

In fact, the finished film seemed so dark to Scorsese—and it was accompanied by a bloodied De Niro boxer poster—that he wondered if anyone would go see it. "The poster with the picture of Bob's face all beat and battered," he said, "I mean if you're a girl, nineteen years old, I don't know if you'd say, 'Let's go see this one.' " [7]

The movie did not win best picture of the year, losing to *Ordinary People*, but respect continued to grow for the work for years afterwards. In 1990, *Raging Bull* was included in the National Film Registry. It was also not a major box office hit, grossing $23 million, though it has continued to rack up views on rentals. The budget for the two-hour, nine-minute film, was $18 million.

"It wasn't a big movie," De Niro said. "It wasn't really a hit. But it was a movie we were proud of." [8]

Eventually, *Raging Bull* became viewed as a modern American movie classic. The American Film Institute has rated *Raging Bull* as the best sports movie of all time. When the institute first ranked the top 100 movies of all time in 1998, *Raging Bull* was listed 24th. In 2007, when the list was updated with a fresh vote, *Raging Bull* was ranked fourth.

The movie opens in 1964 when De Niro/LaMotta is doing one of his solo performances, *An Evening with Jake LaMotta*. To the audience he says, "A horse, a horse, my kingdom for a horse. I haven't had a winner in six months." A little Shakespeare, a little shtick.

There are fight scenes against Jimmy Reeves in Cleveland and Sugar Ray Robinson in Detroit when Jake knocked him through the ropes. Famed ring announcer Don Dunphy calls some of the play by play.

There is a scene where young Jake goes into a rage about the cooking of his steak with his first wife. There is a scene where Vikki tenderly kisses Jakes wounds. Then, he gives her wounds. "I look at somebody the wrong way and I get slapped," she said on screen.

A fight scene from the infamous bout with Billy Fox is included. Lesser known to non-boxing fans is that light-heavyweight champion Eddie Mustapha Muhammad, who later became a well-known trainer, too, played Fox. Fox was supposed to be inept, but Eddie never had such a bad day in the ring in real life.

Notably, a mob guy in the film succinctly summarizes Jake's relationship with the gangsters. The guy says, "The man's got a head of rock."

True, LaMotta had a head of rock when dealing with the mob, stubborn and refusing to cooperate until pushed to the limit. That was him alright with those guys. He also had a head of rock in the ring, and it should be remembered how important it was for him to stay upright, even when taking a beating. In LaMotta's last loss to Robinson, the St. Valentine's Day Massacre, he wrapped one arm in the ropes to keep from going down. In the movie, when the fight ends, De Niro/LaMotta has blood all over his face, but he proudly yells repeatedly, "You never got me down, Ray." That was LaMotta all over, too.

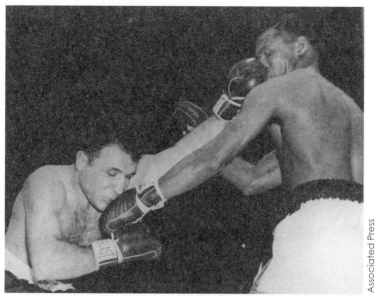

Jake LaMotta and Sugar Ray Robinson fought for the sixth
and last time in Chicago on February 14, 1951 with Robinson
capturing the middleweight crown in a bout called
"The St. Valentine's Day Massacre."

Raging Bull made its premiere in New York City on November 14, 1980. LaMotta wore a tuxedo for the occasion. Vikki, matching him in fancy dress, with a white fur, joined Jake for the opening, along with son Jake Jr. Beginning on this night, and for some time following, Vikki became known in media circles as "Mrs. Raging Bull." Jake's other wives lost out. That was because Vikki was the female core of the movie based on the timing of her marriage with LaMotta and how it overlapped his fight career.

Jake and Vikki, seated with the Hollywood folks, watched the film unfold. Riveted by the portrayal, Jake seemed at last to realize how he was going to look to the world outside of the ring. The story goes that he turned to Vikki and said, "Was I really that bad?" And she responded by saying, "You were worse." [9]

Jake recognized immediately that he had been portrayed as an unsympathetic character, but he was not vociferous in defending himself. Nor, he learned as time passed, was he held to any account for the negative behavior shown in the movie. What resonated more than anything with the public again, really two generations removed from his prime boxing days, was his name.

When Jake LaMotta showed up to do a stage show, people mostly remembered that he was a former world champion fighter and a movie had been made about him. It worked out pretty well for him in the ensuing years. Even the nickname, "Raging Bull," had cachet. Although the title was meant to be all-encompassing, Jake in the ring and Jake out of the ring, Jake pummeling foes with his fists and Jake's torment in his mind, the name was more routinely applied retroactively to his boxing days, commonly applied as a general description of his ring demeanor.

Maybe LaMotta's feelings were a little bit hurt in the beginning, but this was his golden goose and he knew it. He gladly went on tour to promote the movie, and with the passage of time, he grew to appreciate the film, at least what it did for him, more and more.

Numerous times he was asked what he thought of the film and he was able to tailor his response in a general way.

"*Raging Bull* happens to be one of the best movies of the 1980s," LaMotta once said. "I think *Raging Bull* is one of the best fight pictures of all-time. And the film made me a champion all over again." [10]

It did so by rekindling his name before the public and reminding people that once he had been the best middleweight boxer in the world. For those things, he was grateful.

Epilogue

One by one they died off, the boxing champions of the 1940s, but Jake LaMotta persevered. He went on beyond becoming a senior citizen, beyond his 70s and 80s into his 90s. Some might think anyone of that age would be a home-body, would never go out, and never travel. But to the best of his ability, LaMotta continued to make appearances at autograph shows, and he made special trips from New York City to upstate Canastota, New York, outside of Syracuse in June of 2016 and June of 2017 where the International Boxing Hall of Fame is located.

LaMotta came for the annual Hall induction ceremony, just a few weeks before his birthday. He knew the place well enough. The small-town home honoring boxing's greats had been his destination before, both as a visitor and an induct-ee. LaMotta was enshrined in the Hall in 1990.

Unlike the blown-up LaMotta pictured at the end of the movie *Raging Bull*, later in life LaMotta slimmed down. He was even skinnier than his fighting weight. He also had taken to wearing a cowboy hat regularly.

Although he had not thrown a real punch in anger in some time, in the years after he turned 90, LaMotta was known to shadow box as a way of staying fit. And as long as he could talk and his mind was sharp, LaMotta kept acting. He appeared in 17 movies altogether, in addition to TV shows and some commercials. He seemed to enjoy live performances the most. As recently as 2012 with the help of his last wife, Denise Baker, LaMotta engaged in a modestly produced, 50-minute-long play named *The Lady and The Champ*. Besides LaMotta, the other characters are a reporter interviewing him, and Baker. He was 90 years old at the time and still enthralled with show business. However, the show did not gain good reviews. It was denounced as being poorly conceived, although the *New York Times* gave LaMotta special praise for his handling of the I-coulda-been-a-contendah Marlon Brando speech from the film *On the Waterfront*.

When it comes to jokes, LaMotta had a storage vault in his head, but he also repeated stories and comments often upon meeting reporters or while talking on stage. An old one followed the release of *Raging Bull* where he told the producers he wanted to play himself, but they supposedly said, "Jake, you're not the type." [1]

Although LaMotta never considered his encounter with Billy Fox and the mob to be a laughing matter, at least once, he did make a joke about it, saying, "You win some, you throw some." [2]

Long after he finished boxing, *Raging Bull* kept LaMotta going. It kept him in the limelight fielding interviews. He repeated himself in many of them, but he also sounded downright introspective or at least philosophical, certainly more so at 80 or 90 than at 30. In his older age, LaMotta gave an interview in which the words seemed to be in direct contrast to how he behaved with his first six wives.

"Most of the time husbands and wives argue about stupid, foolish things," he said. "If it doesn't mean that much to you, give in to your wife. If you don't give in, you're giving in to not having sex." [3]

Jake, the wise man. None of that was advice he ever followed, at least not for six marriages.

Raging jealousy was one of LaMotta's lifelong traits and one can only imagine how he would have reacted if Vikki had decided to pose nude for *Playboy* when they were together or soon after. At 51, *Playboy* sought her out, and although it took quite a bit of convincing, Vikki eventually acquiesced and bared her body in the November 1981 issue.

Jake might well have killed her with his fists if such an event had occurred on his watch.

The funniest part of all was that LaMotta joked about Vikki doing such a thing in a magazine article around the time *Raging Bull* came out. It was his way of complimenting her. Strangely, Jake chimed in seriously, saying she would be great. Was this the Jake LaMotta she knew?

The seed was planted, but Vikki still said no, she wouldn't pose naked. Then she thought about it, thought maybe. Then, it was no again. Then, finally okay. After she posed and the magazine hit the streets, Vikki said older women came up to her to thank her for baring herself at her age because it made them feel better. Guys began hitting on her routinely, though, and she was irritated by that. In addition, all kinds of sex and nudie magazines also approached her to do additional shoots. She shut them down.

After Vikki posed for *Playboy*, Jake invited her to a sports dinner. Once there, she mingled, enjoying her new popularity. Jake watched grouchily from afar and drank heavily. They left together, but in the vehicle as he dropped her off, Jake said, "Goodbye, Vikki, I've lost what little respect I had left for you. I never want to see you again." [4]

"Well, okay," is likely what she thought, although who knows what reason Vikki might have had to go to a social event with a man who had regularly beaten her in the first place.

Over the several days of the International Boxing Hall of Fame events of June 2016, LaMotta was not very visible. He turned out for a light-hearted event at the Rusty Rail Party House, then sat at the head table for the main banquet in the Oncenter in downtown Syracuse. He wore a black cowboy hat and used a cane to walk to his seat, with Denise helping him. LaMotta had a rose in the lapel of his sports coat.

One by one, show-stopping boxers were introduced. This group included Sugar Ray Leonard, Roberto Duran, and Marvin Hagler. The man who got the loudest ovation, a standing ovation, was Jake LaMotta.

It was bewildering to some that LaMotta would seem to be revered more than those famed and acknowledged greats. One man stayed seated while most in the crowd of about 1,000 people stood clapping. Those guys are there and it is LaMotta who gets the standing O? He shook his head. "Don't ask me," he said. He was thinking of the ugly parts of LaMotta's past, being jailed, throwing a fight, and the beating his wives. The public seemed to have amnesia.

"I don't want to go there," said the anonymous sportswriter.[5]

Many former fighters who attended were amazed to see LaMotta as mobile as he seemed to be at 93, going on 94.

"I hope I'll be that guy and be that active when I'm old," said one-time cruiserweight champion Marvin Camel, who was 64. "He's still got his memory. I want to be in the shape he is as old as he is. Or as young as he is."[6]

That evening Carlos Ortiz, then 79 and winner of the lightweight world championship and the super-lightweight crown, much like Camel, was astonished by LaMotta's seeming vigor and the fact that he was even still alive.

"I wish I could be that way," said Ortiz, of Ponce, Puerto Rico. "It's beautiful. It's gorgeous. It's amazing." Given that LaMotta was a brawler, a fighter who bore in and also took a considerable amount of punches, yet still fought 106 times and was still present and accounted for, was also something Ortiz marveled at. "It's not an intelligent way to fight. But he was a smart fighter. He was always in good condition. He got away with it because of his guts. He was a great fighter. The way he fought, not many guys lasted."[7]

When the dinner broke up, fans were invited up to the head table to obtain autographs. The crowd in front of LaMotta was of a good size. He sat still, signing Hall of Fame programs with deliberate penmanship. Baker sat with him. Each autograph seeker thrust out a program or a sheet of paper, saying he was glad to meet him. LaMotta did not speak to them, concentrating on writing. But periodically, he shook hands with those who waited to meet him.

In a magazine interview once, LaMotta was asked whom he thought were the best middleweight fighters of all time. "I would say definitely Sugar Ray Robinson," he said, "and Marcel Cerdan. And, of course, me. I'm there also." He laughed when he said it, but LaMotta probably meant it.[8]

The question is how the rest of the world views his stature. *The Ring* magazine ranked him in its top 10 in the 160-pound division. *The Ring, Boxing News,* and other observers granted LaMotta high marks for owning one of the best chins of all time. That's why, apparently, he was so difficult to knock out. A website called *The Pugil List* ranked LaMotta ninth all-time in the middleweight class. *Box Rec,* the statistical record keeper, listed LaMotta fifth in 2001.

Long-time Philadelphia boxing promoter J. Russell Peltz, another Hall of Famer, never saw LaMotta fight live, but he believes LaMotta makes a good case for being thought of highly in the division. He heard LaMotta say of his series with Robinson, whom many believe is the best pound-for-pound fighter of all, "I fought him six times and most of the fights were pretty close. Where does that leave me?" Given what Peltz has read about some of LaMotta's hard living, he added, "It's amazing he's still alive."[9]

Another boxing figure with a well-honed sense of history is Hall of Famer Harold Lederman, the HBO TV judge, as well as a long-time ringside judge. "I think he's maybe about sixth," Lederman said of LaMotta's all-time standing amongst middleweights. "He was aggressive. He was always moving in. He took a great punch. If Sugar Ray couldn't knock him out, nobody could." [10]

Whenever LaMotta appeared in a show or at a boxing event, sportswriters wanted to hear his thoughts. His memory was long and his wit was quite respectable when it came to answering their questions. Sometimes the jokes morphed into more serious observations than one might expect. Once, he talked of growing up poor in his New York neighborhood, but he did not put it quite so simply.

"I read the Romans had bread and circuses," LaMotta said. "We had home relief and boxing." [11]

Part of LaMotta's reputation was his toughness and that impression was fueled by what Lederman noted—he never took a step back.

"You're gonna have a strange personality to explain what I did," LaMotta said. "You gotta be strange if you ever did something that's unique. I can't explain it to you. I worked. That's all I can say. It's drive. It's a drive that you can't explain. I can't explain. . . Either you're tough or you're not." [12]

Maybe Jake LaMotta lived long enough to confront the worst moments of his past. Anyone in their 90s probably is aware they are living on borrowed time. They may or may not have regrets. They may or may not indulge in confessions. Chances are it's too late to make it up to everyone who was wronged along the way, even if they wanted to do so.

In a 1988 interview with *Sports Illustrated* when LaMotta was only 66, he did talk as if he had gained a measure of wisdom, speaking the way someone entering old age might when he looked back on such an up-and-down journey.

"I've done it all," LaMotta said. "I went from the top to the bottom, from champion of the world to a chain gang. Then I picked myself up. I made a lot of mistakes, but I tried to correct them. I took one step forward and then another one and it's been a steady grind like that right up to this day." [13]

As someone who abused his body so thoroughly in several ways, it was nearly impossible for Jake LaMotta to think at that time he would still be going, still be signing his name for fans, still be the champ in enough minds to carry on for another 30 years.

Postscript

Jake LaMotta died on September 19, 2017, at the Palm Garden Nursing Home in Aventura, Florida. The cause of death was given as pneumonia.

With an irony the old slugger would have appreciated, many of the obituary stories written about his career as the former middleweight champion of the world incorporated the name of the movie *Raging Bull* into the first sentences of their summation of his life.

Jake LaMotta, age 90, poses for pictures outside the *Mike Tyson: Undisputed Truth* event in New York.

Once famous for being the boxing world's 160-pound champion, LaMotta found renewed fame from the 1980 movie about his life made by Martin Scorsese in which actor Robert De Niro played him in one of his most enduring roles.

"Rest in peace, champ," was the statement De Niro released when he learned of LaMotta's death.

It was announced in 2012 that LaMotta, already in his 90s, took Denise Baker, his long-time companion, as his seventh wife, but at the time of his death, some sources referred to her as his fiancée of 25 years. Others referred to Baker as LaMotta's wife. She was at his side when he passed away after he was admitted to the home for hospice care.

"He was a great man, sensitive, and had eyes that danced right up to the end," Baker said. "I love him. God rest his soul. And he never went down!" [1]

Most of the stories focused on LaMotta's ring life and his achievement of winning 83 fights, as well as his intense and lengthy rivalry with Sugar Ray Robinson. Much of LaMotta's ring reputation was built around his showdowns with Robinson, even though he lost most of them.

One thing he was proud of was how he was impossible to knock down, something noted by Baker. Seemingly forgotten was that near the end of his active career, LaMotta did once drop to the canvas due to the fists of Danny Nardico in a bout on December 31, 1952, in Coral Gables, Florida. LaMotta's furious style is what made him as well-remembered as he was to fight followers.

"To LaMotta, fighting was a personal statement," said Bert Sugar, the flamboyant author and boxing historian, who predeceased LaMotta. "He fought with an anger that seemed as if it would spring forth from the top of his head like a volcanic eruption." [2]

In 1997, *The Ring* named LaMotta as the boxer with the best chin in the 75-year history of its covering the sport. Five years later, in another retrospective, the magazine listed LaMotta 52nd on its list of "The 80 Greatest Fighters of The Past 80 Years," and in its top-10 list of middleweights.

While acknowledging the care and effort that went into making the prize-winning movie about his life, LaMotta was initially uncomfortable with his image portrayed on the big screen. It was all compelling drama, but no one walked out of the theatre thinking LaMotta was a nice guy. "When I saw the film, I was upset," LaMotta said in 1980. "I kind of look bad in it. Then I realized it was true. That's the way it was. I was a no-good bastard. I realize it now. It's not the way I am now, but the way I was then." [3]

While seeing others' view of him made LaMotta reflective, he had also in a less-publicized manner been self-critical about the young man he was before becoming a boxing title-holder. "A good-for-nothing bum kid," he called himself, and one with a bad temper, to boot.[4]

While certainly *Raging Bull* is on the short lists of the greatest movies about boxing, if not the best, Scorsese attempted to employ the metaphor of one tormented man's life to take the story beyond the ring. The degree to which he succeeded no doubt reflects the universal nature of the story while also being one man's personal story.

"I would think that Jake thinks it's a movie about himself," Scorsese said when the movie was new. "But those who think it's a boxing picture would be out of their minds. It's brutal, sure, but it's a brutality that could take place not only in the boxing ring, but in the bedroom or in an office. Jake is an elemental man." [5]

Kevin Mitchell, a boxing writer for *The Guardian* in London, took note of the Scorsese comments when he wrote of LaMotta's passing. "The fine details of his brief reign and the denouement are not always absorbed in recollections of his career, mainly because one of the greatest movies of all time painted him in classically Shakespearean mode, a doomed victim to fear then pity," Mitchell wrote. "Martin Scorsese's *Raging Bull* simultaneously rehabbed LaMotta's standing as a middleweight champion and exposed the essential ugliness of his personality. But his boxing was not the real story." [6]

If the film was character study at its most piercing, boxing had long had its less-than-subtle way of revealing character inside the ropes. While he may have absorbed wisdom along with the body shots to become a bit more well-rounded man later in life and one possessed of introspective qualities he never would have thought of as a young man, it is difficult to believe the LaMotta analysis issued by venerable trainer Ray Arcel could be more pointed. "When he was in the ring, it was like he was in a cage fighting for his life," Arcel said. [7]

Arcel's observation could easily have been transported outside the ring, too. It seemed Jake LaMotta was fighting for his life within some kind of cage every single day: on the street, within his marriages, in the business world, and in show business.

LaMotta was not only survived by Baker and her daughters, but four of his own daughters, two brothers, and two sisters. Daughter Christi LaMotta posted a note similar to De Niro's statement, on Facebook, reading "Rest in Peace, Pop." [8]

Ed Brophy, executive director of The International Boxing Hall of Fame in Canastota, New York, where LaMotta was welcomed annually at its annual induction ceremony and banquets, recalled LaMotta's special traits in the ring. "Jake LaMotta was one of the toughest and most relentless boxers in ring history," Brophy said. "The Hall of Fame joins the boxing world in mourning the passing of a legend." [9]

The Hall of Fame then lowered its American flag to half-staff to honor Jake LaMotta.

Notes

Chapter 1

1. Anderson, Chris, Sharon McGehee, and Jake LaMotta. *Raging Bull II* (Secaucus, New Jersey: Lyle Stuart, Inc., 1986), 8.
2. LaMotta, Jake, Joseph Carter, and Peter Savage. *Raging Bull: My Story* (New York: Da Capo Press, 1997), 2–3.
3. Ibid.
4. Ibid., 57.
5. Ibid., 9.
6. Ibid., 13.
7. Ibid., 22.
8. Ibid.

Chapter 2

1. LaMotta, Jake, Joseph Carter, and Peter Savage. *Raging Bull: My Story* (New York: Da Capo Press, 1997), 41.
2. Ibid., 43.
3. Ibid., 45.
4. Ibid., 64.

Chapter 3

1. LaMotta, Jake, Joseph Carter, and Peter Savage. *Raging Bull: My Story* (New York: Da Capo Press, 1997), 75.
2. Ibid., 89.
3. Ibid., 91–92.

Chapter 5

1. LaMotta, Jake, Joseph Carter, and Peter Savage. *Raging Bull: My Story* (New York: Da Capo Press, 1997), 112.
2. Haygood, Wil. *Sweet Thunder: The Life and Times of Sugar Ray Robinson* (New York: Alfred A. Knopf, 2009), 35.
3. Robinson, Sugar Ray, and Dave Anderson. *Sugar Ray* (New York: The Viking Press, 1969), 75.
4. Ibid., 7.
5. Ibid., 88.
6. Ibid., 112.

Chapter 6

1. Robinson, Sugar Ray, and Dave Anderson. *Sugar Ray* (New York: The Viking Press, 1969), 108.
2. Ibid., 108.
3. LaMotta, Jake, Joseph Carter, and Peter Savage. *Raging Bull: My Story* (New York: Da Capo Press, 1997), 113.
4. Robinson, Sugar Ray, and Dave Anderson. *Sugar Ray* (New York: The Viking Press, 1969), 109.
5. Ibid., 109.
6. Ibid., 110.
7. LaMotta, Jake, Joseph Carter, and Peter Savage. *Raging Bull: My Story* (New York: Da Capo Press, 1997), 119.
8. "Robinson Gets off Floor to Win," *Associated Press*, 26 February 1943.
9. LaMotta, Jake, Joseph Carter, and Peter Savage. *Raging Bull: My Story* (New York: Da Capo Press, 1997), 119.

Chapter 7

1. LaMotta, Jake, Joseph Carter, and Peter Savage. *Raging Bull: My Story* (New York: Da Capo Press, 1997), 109.
2. Ibid.
3. Ibid., 110.
4. Ibid., 123.
5. Ibid.
6. LaMotta, Vikki, and Thomas Hauser. *Knockout!: The Sexy, Violent, Extraordinary Life of Vikki LaMotta* (Toronto, Canada: Sport Classic Books, 2006), 36.
7. Ibid., 55.
8. Ibid.
9. Ibid., 53.
10. Ibid.
11. LaMotta, Jake, Joseph Carter, and Peter Savage. Raging Bull: My Story (New York: Da Capo Press, 1997), 123.
12. Ibid.
13. Ibid.

Chapter 8

1. LaMotta, Jake, Joseph Carter, and Peter Savage. *Raging Bull: My Story* (New York: Da Capo Press, 1997), 120.
2. Fleischer, Nat. "Hail Zivic, LaMotta," *The Ring*, April 1943.
3. LaMotta, Jake, Joseph Carter, and Peter Savage. *Raging*

Bull: My Story (New York: Da Capo Press, 1997), 120.
4. Ibid.
5. Ibid., 121.
6. Ibid.
7. Haygood, Wil. *Sweet Thunder: The Life and Times of Sugar Ray Robinson* (New York: Alfred A. Knopf, 2009), 228.
8. Ibid.,
9. Ibid., 229.

Chapter 9

1. LaMotta, Jake, Joseph Carter, and Peter Savage. *Raging Bull: My Story* (New York: Da Capo Press, 1997), 159.
2. Ibid., 161.
3. Ibid.
4. Ibid., 162.

Chapter 10

1. LaMotta, Jake, Joseph Carter, and Peter Savage. *Raging Bull: My Story* (New York: Da Capo Press, 1997), 133.
2. Ibid.
3. LaMotta, Vikki, and Thomas Hauser. *Knockout!: The Sexy, Violent, Extraordinary Life of Vikki LaMotta* (Toronto, Canada: Sport Classic Books, 2006), 57.
4. Ibid., 62.
5. Ibid.
6. Ibid..
7. Ibid., 64.
8. Ibid., 65.
9. Ibid.
10. Ibid., 68.
11. Ibid.

Chapter 11

1. *La Vie En Rose*, 2007.
2. LaMotta, Jake, Joseph Carter, and Peter Savage. *Raging Bull: My Story* (New York: Da Capo Press, 1997), 166.
3. Albertani, Francis. "Jake LaMotta Heads List of Middleweight Title Contenders," *The Ring*, November 1946.
4. Ibid.
5. Ibid.

Chapter 12

1. LaMotta, Vikki, and Thomas Hauser. *Knockout!: The Sexy, Violent, Extraordinary Life of Vikki LaMotta* (Toronto, Canada: Sport Classic Books, 2006), 70.
2. Ibid., 71.
3. Ibid., 71–72.
4. LaMotta, Jake, Joseph Carter, and Peter Savage. *Raging Bull: My Story* (New York: Da Capo Press, 1997), 163.
5. Albertani, Francis. "Jake LaMotta Heads List of Middleweight Title Contenders," *The Ring*, November 1946.

Chapter 13

1. LaMotta, Vikki, and Thomas Hauser. *Knockout!: The Sexy, Violent, Extraordinary Life of Vikki LaMotta* (Toronto, Canada: Sport Classic Books, 2006), 75.
2. Fleischer, Nat. "Title Regained by U.S.," *The Ring*, August 1949.
3. LaMotta, Jake, Joseph Carter, and Peter Savage. *Raging Bull: My Story* (New York: Da Capo Press, 1997), 165.
4. Fleischer, Nat. "Title Regained by U.S.," *The Ring*, August 1949.
5. Unknown. (1949 June 15). *Jake LaMotta-Marcel Cerdan*, Retrieved from YouTube.
6. Dawson, James P. "LaMotta Wins Title by Knockout as Cerdan Is Unable to Answer Bell For 10th," *The New York Times*, 17 June 1949.
7. Unknown. (1949 June 15). *Jake LaMotta-Marcel Cerdan*, Retrieved from YouTube.
8. Ibid.
9. Dawson, James P. "LaMotta Wins Title by Knockout as Cerdan Is Unable to Answer Bell For 10th," *The New York Times*, 17 June 1949.
10. Ibid.
11. Fleischer, Nat. "Title Regained by U.S.," *The Ring*, August 1949.
12. LaMotta, Vikki, and Thomas Hauser. *Knockout!: The Sexy, Violent, Extraordinary Life of Vikki LaMotta* (Toronto, Canada: Sport Classic Books, 2006), 76.
13. Ibid., 76.
14. LaMotta, Jake, Joseph Carter, and Peter Savage. *Raging Bull: My Story* (New York: Da Capo Press, 1997), 169.
15. Ibid.

Chapter 14

1. Marcus, Norman. "We'll Always Have Paris," boxing.com (accessed on 16 May 2012).
2. LaMotta, Jake, Joseph Carter, and Peter Savage. Raging Bull: My Story (New York: Da Capo Press, 1997), 171.
3. Ibid. 170.
4. Ibid.
5. Ibid.,171.
6. Fleischer, Nat. "Title Regained by U.S.," *The Ring*, August 1949.
7. Ibid.
8. Ibid.
9. LaMotta, Vikki, and Thomas Hauser. *Knockout!: The Sexy, Violent, Extraordinary Life of Vikki LaMotta* (Toronto, Canada: Sport Classic Books, 2006), 77.
10. Ibid.
11. Izenberg, Jerry. "At Large Column: The Other Marcel," *Newark Star-Ledger*, 28 April 1965.
12. Ibid.
13. Ibid.
14. Burke, Carolyn. "No Regrets: The Life of Edith Piaf," (Knopf, New York: 2011), Ekphora.com.
15. Ibid.
16. Ibid.
17. Marcus, Norman. "We'll Always Have Paris," boxing.com (accessed on 16 May 2012).

Chapter 15

1. LaMotta, Vikki, and Thomas Hauser. *Knockout!: The Sexy, Violent, Extraordinary Life of Vikki LaMotta* (Toronto, Canada: Sport Classic Books, 2006), 77.
2. Ibid.
3. LaMotta, Jake, Joseph Carter, and Peter Savage. *Raging Bull: My Story* (New York: Da Capo Press, 1997), 178.
4. Ibid.
5. Bogs, Bill. *Boxers Round Table Mid-Day with Bill Boggs*, (TV Show retrieved from YouTube May 3, 2012).
6. Ibid.

Chapter 16

1. LaMotta, Jake, Joseph Carter, and Peter Savage. *Raging Bull: My Story* (New York: Da Capo Press, 1997), 179.

2. Ibid., 181.
3. Ibid.
4. "Best Come from Behind Win," *The Ring*, February 1951.
5. Daniel, Daniel M. "LaMotta-Dauthuille Cited Fight of the Year," *The Ring*, February 1951.
6. Ibid.
7. Ibid.
8. Ibid.

Chapter 17

1. Haygood, Wil. *Sweet Thunder: The Life and Times of Sugar Ray Robinson* (New York: Alfred A. Knopf, 2009), 124.
2. Robinson, Sugar Ray, and Dave Anderson. *Sugar Ray* (New York: The Viking Press, 1969), 136.
3. Ibid., 137.
4. LaMotta, Vikki, and Thomas Hauser. *Knockout!: The Sexy, Violent, Extraordinary Life of Vikki LaMotta* (Toronto, Canada: Sport Classic Books, 2006), 81.
5. Ibid.
6. Smith, Red. "Views of Sport: The Dawn Patrol," *New York Herald-Tribune*, 15 February 1951.
7. Abramson, Jesse. "LaMotta, at 160, Holds 4½-Pound Edge Over Robinson," *New York Herald-Tribune*, 15 February 1951.
8. LaMotta, Vikki, and Thomas Hauser. *Knockout!: The Sexy, Violent, Extraordinary Life of Vikki LaMotta* (Toronto, Canada: Sport Classic Books, 2006), 83.
9. LaMotta, Jake, Joseph Carter, and Peter Savage. *Raging Bull: My Story* (New York: Da Capo Press, 1997), 187.

Chapter 18

1. LaMotta, Vikki, and Thomas Hauser. *Knockout!: The Sexy, Violent, Extraordinary Life of Vikki LaMotta* (Toronto, Canada: Sport Classic Books, 2006), 85.
2. Ibid., 87.
3. LaMotta, Jake, Joseph Carter, and Peter Savage. *Raging Bull: My Story* (New York: Da Capo Press, 1997), 187.
4. Mitchell, Kevin. "The Vikki LaMotta Story: Jake, Raging Bull, Playboy, Sinatra and the Mob," *The Guardian*, 25 September 2010.
5. LaMotta, Jake, Joseph Carter, and Peter Savage. *Raging Bull: My Story* (New York: Da Capo Press, 1997), 187–188.